Interview Guide for Evaluating DSM-IV Psychiatric Disorders and the Mental Status Examination

Mark Zimmerman, M.D.

Associate Professor of Psychiatry & Human Behavior
Brown University
Director, Primary Care Psychiatry Research Program
Rhode Island Hospital
Providence, Rhode Island

*P*sych *P*roducts *P*ress
East Greenwich, RI

Printed in the United States of America.

ISBN: 0-9633821-3-6

To Caryn, Kyle, and Cali, for all you have given and given up.

TABLE OF CONTENTS

INTRODUCTION

This book provides questions for evaluating psychiatric disorders. DSM-IV lists the disorders and their criteria, but it does not guide the beginner in inquiry for them. Students and clinicians in training are relatively unfamiliar with psychiatric diagnoses, and they cannot possibly remember all of the disorders and their corresponding diagnostic criteria within a short period of study. Moreover, it is not obvious what questions to ask to determine the presence of many of the symptoms of mental disorders. How do you inquire for thought withdrawal, delusions of reference, panic attacks, obsessions, identity disturbance, mood instability, etc.? Even more basic, how do you begin the interview?

This book is a guide for evaluating psychiatric disorders. It consists of questions for the most common DSM-IV Axis I diagnoses and all of the Axis II personality disorders. This book is not a standardized interview, to be started on page x and followed until page xx. Rather it is a quick reference to be used in the context of a clinical interview. If a patient complains of depression, the interviewer can turn to the section on major depression and assess the relevant symptoms. If there is a suggestion of excessive drug or alcohol use, the interviewer can refer to the long list of questions for diagnosing drug and alcohol abuse/dependence.

The book contains 9 sections. First, is a listing of the components of a complete psychiatric evaluation. This is followed by a brief section on how to begin a psychiatric interview. Sections 3, 4, and 5 include questions to assess the most common Axis I adult and childhood disorders and all of the Axis II disorders. In section 6, I describe the mental status examination and provide a standardized outline for its' charting and oral presentation. Also included is the mini-mental state exam which should be a part of every psychiatric evaluation. Section 7 is a glossary of commonly used psychiatric terms, and the final two sections include a brief psychosocial interview and a current psychosocial functioning assessment.

The book is organized by diagnosis. Listed in the box at the beginning of each section are the DSM-IV diagnostic rules--which and how many criteria must be present (inclusion criteria) and absent (exclusion criteria) for the diagnosis to be made. For the Axis I disorders, the initial questions in each section can be considered screening questions. If these screening questions are answered negatively, then it is reasonable to skip the remaining questions in the section.

The exception to the diagnosis-based organization of the guide is for five psychotic disorders--schizophrenia, delusional disorder, schizoaffective disorder, schizophreniform disorder, and brief psychotic disorder. Questions to assess delusions and hallucinations are given in one section, and differential diagnosis is outlined and discussed.

The guide should be used in conjunction with the DSM-IV manual or Mini-D. For most diagnoses covered in the guide, the DSM-IV criteria (or a slight abbreviation of them) precede the relevant questions. However, the criteria are not included for the five psychotic disorders in the "Schizophrenia and Other Psychotic Disorders" section. Moreover, the DSM-IV manual includes lucid discussions of differential diagnosis.

Most criteria are assessed by several questions, and follow-ups to the initial questions are preceded by phrases typed in bold face such as **IF YES** or **IF NO**. This is a shorthand way of instructing the interviewer to ask additional questions. For example, **IF YES** means that the ensuing questions should be asked only if the response to the preceding one was yes.

Use of this guide does not guarantee competence. Interviewing involves more than the recitation of listed questions. With experience the clinician develops a style that generates a database for making diagnoses, as well as beginning a therapeutic relationship. Psychiatric diagnosis is not just based on responses to questions. It also relies on observation and evaluation of affect, behavior, and cognition (the ABC of the mental status examination). Also, organic causes of symptoms must be ruled out. However, it is difficult to conduct a psychiatric interview if you do not know what questions to ask. That is the primary purpose of this guide.

Acknowledgement -- Semistructured diagnostic interviews have been widely used in psychiatric research during the past 15 years. I have been involved in developing some of these measures, and have been trained in others. The questions in this volume derive, in part, from this experience. Because there are only a limited number of ways to ask about such symptoms as appetite change, sleep disturbance, etc. the questions will resemble the questions from these interviews, and they deserve acknowledgement. Specifically, had not the Renard Diagnostic Interview, Diagnostic Interview Schedule, Schedule for Affective Disorders and Schizophrenia (SADS), Kiddie SADS, Structured Clinical Interview for DSM-III-R, Structured Interview for DSM-IV Personality Disorders, Personality Disorders Examination, and Diagnostic Interview for Personality Disorders not existed, then the present guide would not have been as rich and complete. Of course the *Interview Guide* does not just include a listing of questions, but it also includes an overview and description of the mental status examination, a glossary of psychiatric terms, and a psychosocial history interview. Thus, the *Interview Guide* should help students and beginning clinicians perform a complete psychiatric evaluation.

COMPONENTS OF THE PSYCHIATRIC EVALUATION

Identifying data   (name, sex, age, race, marital status, source of history, reliability of patient as historian)

Chief complaint   (in patient's own words)

History of present illness

Past psychiatric history

Past medical and surgical history

Current medications

Drug allergies

Medical review of systems

Substance use history   (See pages 12-21)

Family history

Psychosocial history   (See pages 132-141)

Mental status exam   (See pages 120-125)

Physical exam

Differential diagnosis

Treatment plan

BEGINNING THE PSYCHIATRIC INTERVIEW

The patient is probably more nervous than you are. Anxiety, which may be a symptom of their illness or due to their concern about speaking to a mental health professional, is the rule. The patient may be paranoid and suspicious of an unfamiliar doctor. They may also be angry because they are not there willingly. Perhaps they have been involuntarily committed, or perhaps a friend, family member, or boss strongly encouraged or coerced them to be evaluated. Thus, it is important to realize that an important purpose of the initial evaluation is to provide support and understanding to the patient, establish a trusting doctor-patient relationship, a by-product of which will be the information necessary to derive a diagnosis and treatment plan. Of course, even the most experienced and skilled clinician cannot achieve this with all patients.

The evaluation should begin by introducing yourself. Refer to the patient by his/her name. Often it is helpful to tell the patient approximately how long the evaluation will take. The initial inquiry should be in a more open-ended, nonstructured manner. After an overview is obtained, more focused symptom oriented questions can be asked. Because most patients have usually spoken to a nurse or social worker before I interview them, I typically begin my evaluation:

> Hello Mr. Jones, I'm Dr. Zimmerman. I know you've already spoken to someone about what's been going on, and I know I'll be repeating some of the questions they already asked, but it's important and helpful for me to hear you tell your story. I would like to talk with you for about 30-45 minute to find out what's been going on.
>
> So tell me, what's been bothering you (going on)?
> How long has this been going on?
> What else has happened?
> You said these problems have been going on since _____, why did you come here today?

The information from these questions should help you determine which domains of psychopathology to explore in greater detail (i.e., which sections of the guide to turn to). If the patient complains of depression, you should ask the questions about major depression and dysthymia on pages 34-39. If the patient described what sounds like an anxiety attack, you should turn to pages 40-43 for questions about panic disorder and agoraphobia. And so on. The most common DSM-IV Axis I disorders are covered on pages 8-68, whereas the questions for the 10 Axis II personality disorders are on pages 87-119. Childhood disorders are covered on pages 70-85.

Axis I Disorders

ANOREXIA NERVOSA

Inclusion: A-D (In men: A-C)
Exclusion: None

(A) **Refusal to maintain body weight at or above a minimally normal weight for age and height (e.g., weight loss leading to maintenance of body weight less than 85% of that expected; or failure to make expected weight gain during period of growth, leading to body weight less than 85% of that expected).**

Has there ever been a time when people gave you a hard time about being too thin or losing too much weight?
Have you ever weighed much less than people thought you should weigh?
   IF YES TO EITHER QUESTION:
      When did this occur? Is this still true?
      What was the lowest you weighed?
      How tall were you (at the time)?
      What do you weigh now?

(B) **Intense fear of gaining weight or becoming fat, even though underweight.**

During the time you weighed less than others thought you should weigh, were you very afraid of gaining weight or becoming fat?

(C) **Disturbance in the way in which one's body weight or shape is experienced, undue influence of body weight or shape on self-evaluation, or denial of the seriousness of the current low body weight.**

During that time, how did you think your body looked?
Did other people say you were thin, but you thought you <u>looked</u> fat or overweight?
Did any part of your body <u>feel</u> fat?
   IF YES: Which one?

Did your weight or the shape of your body have a big effect on your opinion of yourself? **IF YES:** Tell me about that.

How much did you think about the health risks of weighing (LOWEST WEIGHT)? Did anyone tell you that it was not good for your health to be so thin?

(D) In postmenarcheal females, amenorrhea, i.e., the absence of at least three consecutive menstrual cycles. (A woman is considered to have amenorrhea if her periods occur only following hormone, e.g., estrogen, administration).

When you were very thin or losing weight did you start missing some of your menstrual periods?

IF YES: How often?

Did you ever miss 3 in a row?

BULIMIA NERVOSA

Inclusion:	A-D
Exclusion:	E

(A) Recurrent episodes of binge eating as characterized by both: 1) eating, in a discrete period of time (e.g., within any two hour period), an amount of food that is definitely larger than most people would eat during a similar period of time and under similar circumstances, and 2) a sense of lack of control over eating during the episode (e.g., a feeling that one cannot stop eating or control what or how much one is eating).

1) Have you ever gone on eating binges when you ate abnormally large amounts of food over a short period of time?
   IF YES: How much would you eat during a binge?

2) During a binge did you feel you lost control of your eating?

(B) Recurrent inappropriate compensatory behavior in order to prevent weight gain, such as self-induced vomiting; misuse of laxatives, diuretics, enemas, or other medications; fasting; or excessive exercise.

To prevent gaining weight from the binge, would you sometimes...
   ...force yourself to vomit?
   ...go on strict diets or fast afterwards?
   ...use laxatives or water pills?
   ...give yourself an enema?
   ...exercise vigorously?
      IF YES TO ANY: Describe what that was like.

(C) The binge eating and inappropriate compensatory behaviors both occur, on average, at least twice a week for three months.

How often did you binge?

Was there ever a time lasting at least 3 months when you would binge at least twice a week?

How often did you [COMPENSATORY BEHAVIOR]?
Did you ever do this at least twice a week for 3 or more months?

(D) **Self-evaluation is unduly influenced by body shape and weight.**

Did your weight or the shape of your body have a big effect on your opinion of yourself?
   IF YES: Tell me about that.

(E) <u>Exclude</u> **the diagnosis if the symptoms occur exclusively during episodes of anorexia nervosa.**

IF ANOREXIC: Did you also binge and [COMPENSATORY BEHAVIOR] when you weren't underweight like you were when you were [AGE]?

ALCOHOL ABUSE/DEPENDENCE

> Alcohol Dependence: at least 3 from B
> Alcohol Abuse: at least 1 from A, not dependent

<u>Screening Questions</u>

Now I'm going to ask you some questions about your use of alcohol.
What are your drinking habits like?
Was there ever a time in your life when you drank too much?
 IF YES: How old were you?
Has anyone in your family ever said that you were an excessive drinker?
Have friends, a doctor, or anyone else ever said that you drink too much?
Has alcohol ever caused problems for you?
 IF YES: What kind of problems?
      How old were you when you had these problems?

> **If all of the above questions are ANSWERED NO,**
> **the diagnosis of alcohol abuse/dependence is unlikely.**

The following questions deal with the time you were drinking the
most, and having the most problems with your drinking.

A. **Alcohol Abuse:** A maladaptive pattern of alcohol use leading to
clinically significant impairment or distress, as manifested by one or
more of the following occurring within a twelve month period:

(A1) **Recurrent alcohol use resulting in a failure to fulfill major role**
obligations at work, school, or home (e.g., repeated absences or
poor work performance related to alcohol use; alcohol related
absences, suspensions, or expulsions from school; neglect of
children or household).

Because of drinking, how often did you...

....miss work (or school)?
....have trouble at work (or school)?
....get fired (or suspended or expelled from school)?
....not take care of children?
....not cook, clean the house, or go grocery shopping?

(A2) Recurrent alcohol use in situations in which it is physically hazardous (e.g., driving an automobile or operating a machine when impaired by alcohol use).

Did you drive while intoxicated? **IF YES:** How often?

Did you ever drink and then do something that was potentially physically dangerous (e.g., operate machinery)?

(A3) Recurrent alcohol-related legal problems (e.g. arrests for disorderly conduct).

Were you ever arrested for driving under the influence, or disorderly conduct? **IF YES:** How many times?

(A4) Continued alcohol use despite having persistent or recurrent social or interpersonal problems caused or exacerbated by the effects of the alcohol (e.g., arguments with spouse about consequences of intoxication, physical fights).

Because of your drinking did you...
...frequently have problems or arguments with friends or family?
...spend less time with family or friends?
...get separated or divorced?
...get into physical fights?
...get violent?
    IF YES TO ANY: Did you still drink despite these problems?

B.   Alcohol Dependence: A maladaptive pattern of alcohol use, leading to clinically significant impairment or distress, as manifested by three or more of the following, occurring at any time in the same twelve month period:

(B1) Tolerance, as defined by either: 1) a need for markedly increased amounts of alcohol to achieve intoxication or desired effect, or 2) markedly diminished effect with continued use of the same amount of alcohol.

1) Over time did you drink a lot more to get high or get the same effect as before? **IF YES:** How much more?

2) Did you develop a tolerance to alcohol so that the same amount as previously did not have the same effect?

(B2) **Withdrawal, as manifested by either: 1) within several hours to a few days after cessation or reduction of heavy and prolonged alcohol use, person experienced at least two characteristic symptoms of withdrawal, or 2) alcohol (or related substance) taken to relieve or avoid withdrawal symptoms.**

    1) Did any of the following occur when you quit or cut down your drinking:
            1) Heart racing or sweating
            2) The shakes
            3) Sleep problems
            4) Nausea or vomiting
            5) Seeing, hearing or feeling things that weren't really there (hallucinations)
            6) Feeling fidgety, restless, or agitated
            7) Anxiety or nervousness
            8) Seizures
            __ **IF YES TO ANY:** How soon after you quit or cut down did the [SYMPTOM] begin?

    2) Did you often drink or take anything else to stop withdrawal symptoms, or to prevent them from coming on? (Did you drink in the morning to keep withdrawal symptoms from coming on?)

(B3) **Alcohol is often taken in larger amounts or over a longer period than the person intended.**

When you drank, did you often drink more than you had planned?

When you drank, did you often drink for more time than you had planned?

(B4) **Persistent desire or unsuccessful efforts to cut down or control alcohol use.**

Did you frequently think about cutting down or stopping drinking?
    IF YES: How much did you think about that?
            For how long did you think about that? (Week? Months?)

At times, did you try to cut down or stop but couldn't?
    IF NO: For example, some people try to control their drinking by promising not to begin before a certain time or not to drink alone. Did you ever do things like that?
    IF YES: How often would you try to cut back or stop completely?

(B5) A great deal of time is spent in activities necessary to get alcohol
(e.g., driving long distances), drinking alcohol, or recovering from its
effects.

Did you spend a lot of time doing things and planning ways to get
alcohol?   **IF YES:** Was this the number one thing on your mind?

How much time did you spend drinking?

How often were you intoxlcated?

Did you spend a lot of time recovering from hangovers?

(B6) Important social, occupational, or recreational activities given up or
reduced because of alcohol use.

Did you spend so much of your time drinking that you...
  ...missed a lot of time from work?
  ...spent less time with family or friends?
  ...gave up some hobbies or other interests?
    IF YES: Tell me about that.

(B7) Continued alcohol use despite knowledge of having had a persistent
or recurrent physical or psychological problem that was likely to
have been caused or exacerbated by the alcohol (e.g., continued
drinking despite recognition that an ulcer was made worse by the
alcohol consumption).

Did drinking cause physical problems?
  IF YES: Like what?
      Did you continue to drink despite these problems?

Did drinking cause anxiety or depression?
  IF YES: Did you still drink anyway?

Did drinking cause any other type of psychological problem?
  IF YES: Like what?
      Did you continue to drink despite these problems?

DRUG ABUSE/DEPENDENCE

Drug Dependence: at least 3 from B
Drug Abuse: at least 1 from A, not dependent

<u>Screening Questions</u>

Street Drugs

Have you ever used any street drugs?
  IF YES: What? How frequently?

> *****IF USED LESS THAN 10 TIMES IN LIFE, SKIP TO SCREENING QUESTIONS REGARDING PRESCRIBED MEDICINES*****

> Did you ever think that you used drugs too much?
>   IF YES: How old were you?
> Has anyone in your family ever said that you've used drugs too much?
> Have friends, a doctor, or anyone else ever said that you used drugs too much?
> Have drugs ever caused problems for you?
>   IF YES: What kinds of problems?
>   How old were you when you had these problems?

Prescribed Medication

Have you ever used sleeping pills, tranquilizers, weight loss medicines, or painkillers?
  IF YES: How long did you take [DRUG]?
      Did you get hooked or addicted to it?
      Did you ever take much more than was prescribed?

**If all of the above questions are ANSWERED NO,
the diagnosis of drug abuse/dependence is unlikely.**

The following questions deal with the time you were using drugs the most, and having the most problems with your drug use.

A.   <u>Drug Abuse:</u> **A maladaptive pattern of drug use leading to clinically significant impairment or distress, as manifested by one or more of the following occurring within a twelve month period:**

(A1) **Recurrent drug use resulting in a failure to fulfill major role obligations at work, school, or home (e.g., repeated absences or poor work performance related to drug use; drug related absences, suspensions, or expulsions from school; neglect of children or household).**

Because of your [DRUG] use, how often did you...
....miss work (or school)?
....have trouble at work (or school)?
....get fired (or suspended or expelled from school)?
....not take care of children?
....not cook, clean the house, or go grocery shopping?

(A2) **Recurrent drug use in situations in which it is physically hazardous (e.g., driving an automobile or operating a machine when impaired by drug use).**

Did you frequently drive while high on drugs? **IF YES:** How often?

Did you ever use drugs and then do something that was potentially physically dangerous (e.g., operate machinery)?

(A3) **Recurrent drug-related legal problems.**

Were you ever arrested or busted for using or selling drugs?
   IF YES: How many times?

(A4) **Continued drug use despite having persistent or recurrent social or interpersonal problems caused or exacerbated by the effects of the drug use (e.g., arguments with spouse about consequences of drug use, physical fights).**

Because of your [DRUG] use did you...
...frequently have problems or arguments with friends or family?
...spend less time with family or friends?
...get separated or divorced?
...get into physical fights?
   IF YES TO ANY: Did you still use drugs despite these problems?

B.   <u>Drug Dependence</u>: A maladaptive pattern of drug use, leading to clinically significant impairment or distress, as manifested by three or more of the following, occurring at any time in the same twelve month period:

(B1)   Tolerance, as defined by <u>either</u>: 1) a need for markedly increased amount of the drug to achieve intoxication or desired effect, or 2) markedly diminished effect with continued use of the same amount of the drug.

    1)   Over time did you use a lot more to get high or get the same effect as before? **IF YES:** How much more?

    2)   Did you develop a tolerance to [DRUG] so that the same amount as previously did not have the same effect?

* *
    NOTE: Criterion B2 refers to withdrawal from substances. Withdrawal symptoms vary according to the class of substance. Below, questions are separately listed to determine withdrawal from three classes of substances-- stimulants, opioids, and sedatives.
* *

(B2)   <u>Amphetamine/stimulant or cocaine withdrawal</u>, as manifested by <u>either</u>: 1) within a few hours to several days after cessation or reduction of prolonged and heavy stimulant and cocaine use, person experienced dysphoric mood (item 1), and at least two other characteristic symptoms of withdrawal, or 2) substance (or related substance) often taken to relieve or avoid withdrawal symptoms.

    1)   Did any of the following occur when you quit or cut down on your use of [SUBSTANCE]:
        1)   Depressed, irritable, or anxious mood
        2)   Fatigue
        3)   Vivid, unpleasant dreams
        4)   Increased or decreased sleep
        5)   Increased appetite
        6)   Feeling very slowed down like you were stuck in mud, or the reverse, feeling restless and agitated
            IF YES TO ANY: How soon after you quit or cut down did the [SYMPTOM] begin?
    2)   Did you often use drugs to stop withdrawal symptoms or to prevent them from coming on?

(B2) <u>Opioid withdrawal</u>, as manifested by <u>either</u>: 1) within minutes to a few days after cessation or reduction of prolonged and heavy opioid use, or administration of an opioid antagonist, person experienced at least three characteristic symptoms of withdrawal, or 2) substance often taken to relieve or avoid withdrawal symptoms.

---

1) Did any of the following occur when you quit or cut down on your use of [SUBSTANCE]:
   1) Depressed or irritable mood
   2) Nausea or vomiting
   3) Muscle aches
   4) Tearing or runny nose
   5) Dilated pupils, goose bumps, or sweating
   6) Diarrhea
   7) Yawning
   8) Fever
   9) Decreased sleep
      IF YES TO ANY: How soon after you quit or cut down did the [SYMPTOM] begin?
2) Did you often use drugs to stop withdrawal symptoms or to prevent them from coming on?

(B2) <u>Sedative, hypnotic, or anxiolytic withdrawal</u>, as manifested by <u>either</u>: 1) within several hours to a few days after cessation or reduction of prolonged and heavy substance use, person experienced at least two characteristic symptoms of withdrawal, or 2) substance often taken to relieve or avoid withdrawal symptoms.

---

1) Did any of the following occur when you quit or cut down on your use of [SUBSTANCE]:
   1) Heart racing or sweating
   2) The shakes
   3) Sleep problems
   4) Nausea or vomiting
   5) Seeing, hearing, or feeling things that weren't really there (hallucinations)
   6) Feeling fidgety, restless, or agitated
   7) Anxiety or nervousness
   8) Seizures
      IF YES TO ANY: How soon after you quit or cut down did the [SYMPTOM] begin?
2) Did you often use drugs, or drink alcohol, to stop withdrawal symptoms or to prevent them from coming on?

(B3) **The drug is often taken in larger amounts or over a longer period than the person intended.**

When you used [DRUG], did you often use more than you had planned?

When you used [DRUG], did you often use it for a longer period of time than you had planned?

(B4) **Persistent desire or unsuccessful efforts to cut down or control drug use.**

Did you frequently think about cutting down or stopping your use of [DRUG]? **IF YES:** How much did you think about that?

At times, did you try to cut down or stop but couldn't?
   IF NO: For example, some people try to control their drug use by promising not to begin before a certain time or not to use drugs alone. Did you ever do things like that?
   IF YES: How often would you try to cut back or stop completely?

(B5) **A great deal of time is spent in activities necessary to get drugs (e.g., visiting multiple doctors, driving long distances), using drugs, or recovering from its effects.**

Did you spend a lot of time doing things and planning ways to get drugs? **IF YES:** Was this the number one thing on your mind?

How much time did you spend using [DRUG]?

How often were you high?

Did you spend a lot of time recovering from using [DRUG]?

(B6) **Important social, occupational, or recreational activities given up or reduced because of drug use.**

Did you spend so much of your time getting high that you...
   ...missed a lot of time from work?
   ...spent less time with family or friends?
   ...gave up some hobbies or other interests?
      IF YES: Tell me about that.

(B7) **Continued drug use despite knowledge of having had a persistent or recurrent physical or psychological problem that was likely to have been caused or exacerbated by the drugs (e.g., continued cocaine use despite recognition of cocaine-induced depression).**

Did using [DRUG] cause physical problems?
   IF YES: Like what?
          Did you continue to use [DRUG] despite these problems?

Did using [DRUG] cause anxiety or depression?
   IF YES: Did you still use [DRUG] anyway?

Did using [DRUG] cause any other type of psychological problem?
   IF YES: Like what?
          Did you continue to use [DRUG] despite these problems?

SCHIZOPHRENIA AND OTHER PSYCHOTIC DISORDERS

The diagnostic criteria for schizophrenia are complex and involve 1) inquiry for delusions and hallucinations, 2) inquiry for manic and depressive syndromes and if these have been present, then determining whether they are brief relative to the duration of illness, 3) inquiry for the duration of the active psychotic symptom phase, as well as the residual and prodromal illness phases, 4) inquiry to determine deterioration in level of functioning, and 5) observation of affective, behavioral, and cognitive signs of the illness.

The questions for detecting delusions and hallucinations are listed on pages 26-29. Questions regarding manic and depressive syndromes can be found on pages 30-33 and 34-37, respectively. Many of the prodromal/residual phase symptoms are similar to the schizotypal personality disorder criteria, and the relevant questions are on pages 92-95.

The user of this guide should refer to the DSM-IV manual to fully appreciate the differences between schizophrenia, delusional disorder, schizophreniform disorder, brief psychotic disorder and schizoaffective disorder. The common thread to these disorders is the presence of psychosis. The specific delusions and hallucinations are defined in the glossary. Unlike the other sections of this guide, the questions do not follow the DSM-IV diagnostic algorithms. Instead, I briefly summarize the salient features of these disorders, and then highlight differential diagnosis considerations for five pairs of disorders.

<u>Schizophrenia</u> is generally a chronic illness beginning before the age of 25 in which the individual does not return to his or her premorbid level of functioning. Prominent hallucinations or bizarre delusions are usually present. The person must be ill at least six months, though they need not be actively psychotic all of the time. Three phases of the illness are defined. The prodrome phase refers to a deterioration in function prior to the onset of the active psychotic phase. The active phase symptoms (delusions, hallucinations, disorganized speech, grossly disorganized behavior, or negative symptoms such as flat affect) must be present for at least one month. The residual phase follows the active phase. The features of the residual and prodromal phases include functional impairment, and abnormalities in affect, cognition, and communication. If a manic or depressive syndrome occurs, its duration is brief relative to the duration of the active phase of schizophrenia. (DSM-IV does not indicate how short the mood syndrome must be to be considered "brief".

I will not diagnose schizophrenia if a full mood syndrome has been present during more than 10-20% of the active phase of the illness.)

The DSM-IV definition of schizophrenia has 5 criteria. Criterion A, or the active phase of illness, requires the presence of <u>two</u> of the following features for at least one month: delusions, hallucinations, disorganized speech, grossly disorganized or catatonic behavior, and negative symptoms. Of note, only one of these features is required if the delusions are bizarre, or if there are auditory hallucinations consisting of either a voice keeping up a running commentary on the person's behavior or thoughts, or two or more voices conversing with each other. Criterion B refers to social or occupational impairment, and Criterion C refers to the six month duration of disturbance. Criteria D and E exclude the diagnosis if there is significant mood disorder pathology, or if the disturbance is due to the effects of street drugs, medication, or medical illness.

<u>Delusional Disorder</u> is also usually a chronic illness. The delusions last at least a month and are <u>not</u> bizarre but instead involve situations that can occur in real life such as infidelity, being followed, illness, etc. Hallucinations, if present, are not prominent. Functional impairment is directly linked to the delusional system. Often functioning is not markedly and pervasively impaired. If a manic or depressive syndrome occurs, its duration is brief relative to the duration of the delusions.

<u>Brief Psychotic Disorder</u> requires the presence of <u>one</u> of the following for at least one day but less than a month: delusions, hallucinations, disorganized speech, or grossly disorganized or catatonic behavior. The individual returns to his or her normal self.

<u>Schizophreniform Disorder</u> lasts at least one month, but less than six months, is characterized by delusions, prominent hallucinations, or the other active phase features of schizophrenia, and a manic or depressive syndrome, if present, must be brief relative to the duration of the psychotic symptoms. Thus, the criteria are similar to those of schizophrenia except the illness duration is less than six months, and there is no social or occupational impairment requirement.

<u>Schizoaffective Disorder</u> is diagnosed when the patient has the characteristic features of the active phase of schizophrenia, but the duration of the manic or depressive syndrome is <u>not</u> brief relative to the duration of the psychosis. However, for at least two weeks the individual has delusions or hallucinations but not prominent mood symptoms (and this excludes the diagnosis of a mood disorder).

DIFFERENTIATING PSYCHOTIC DISORDERS

1. **Schizophrenia vs. Delusional Disorder:** In delusional disorder, the content of the delusions involves events that may actually occur to some people in real life (e.g., being followed by the FBI, having cancer, becoming a famous entertainer or author, being poisoned etc.). Bizarre delusions such as thought broadcasting and delusions of control, and prominent hallucinations, only occur in schizophrenia. Hallucinations can occur in individuals with delusional disorder; however, they are limited to a few brief periods. Similarly, disorganized speech, grossly disorganized or catatonic behavior, and negative symptoms are usually absent in delusional disorder (or if present, they are present for less than a few hours). Thus, criterion A of schizophrenia is not present. Nonbizarre delusions can occur in schizophrenia; however, they are not the only psychotic symptom. The individual with schizophrenia additionally experiences either bizarre delusions, prominent hallucinations, or markedly disturbed affect, thought processes, or behavior.

2. **Schizophrenia vs. Schizoaffective Disorder:** The psychotic symptoms are the same. In schizoaffective disorder a manic or depressive episode <u>must be present</u>, and the duration of the mood syndrome is <u>not brief</u> relative to the duration of the psychosis. (As noted above, DSM-IV does not define "brief duration.") However, to be diagnosed with schizoaffective disorder there must be at least two weeks in which the delusions or hallucinations are present but prominent mood symptoms are not.

3. **Schizoaffective Disorder vs. Mood Disorder with Psychotic Features:** In a psychotic mood disorder, there are no periods (or only very brief ones) characterized by psychosis but without prominent mood symptoms. You cannot rely on the content and type of psychotic symptoms, or the number and severity of mood symptoms, to distinguish these two disorders. Rather, the distinguishing factor is whether or not the psychotic and mood symptoms overlap in time.

4. **Schizophrenia vs. Schizophreniform Disorder:** The symptom inclusion criteria are the same. The primary difference is that schizophrenia lasts for more than six months (including the prodromal, active, and residual phases), whereas in schizophreniform disorder the pathology (i.e., all three phases) has lasted less than six months.

5. **Schizophreniform Disorder vs. Brief Psychotic Disorder:** Both refer to psychotic disorders of brief duration. The psychotic symptom inclusion criteria are similar, but not identical. The psychosis inclusion criteria are broader for brief psychotic disorder (any one of: delusions, hallucinations, disorganized speech, grossly disorganized behavior or speech <u>versus</u> criterion A of schizophrenia which requires at least two of five features (unless the delusions or hallucinations are of a special nature, in which case only one feature is required)). Schizophreniform disorder lasts at least a month, whereas brief psychotic disorder lasts less than a month.

ASSESSING DELUSIONS AND HALLUCINATIONS

DELUSION OF REFERENCE

When watching TV, listening to the radio, or reading the paper do you notice that they are referring to you, or that there are special messages intended specifically for you?
IF YES: What have you noticed?

Does it seem like strangers on the street are taking special notice of you or talking about you?
IF YES: Is it a feeling you have, or are you pretty sure that they are talking about/referring to you?
IF PRETTY SURE: How do you know?

Do things seem especially arranged for you?
IF YES: In what way?

DELUSION OF PERSECUTION

Is anybody against you, following you, giving you a hard time, or trying to hurt you?
IF YES: Tell me about that.

Do you feel like there's a plot to hurt you?
IF YES: Who's involved?
Why would they want to hurt you?

THOUGHT BROADCASTING

Do you ever think of something so strongly that people could hear your thoughts?
IF YES: So, people can hear what you are thinking even when you're not talking?
How do you know?

DELUSION OF MIND READING

Are people able to read your mind and know what you're thinking?
IF YES: How can they do this?
Can anyone do it, or just some people? Who?
Do they literally read your thoughts, or do they read your facial expression to know what you're thinking?

THOUGHT WITHDRAWAL

Are your thoughts ever taken out of your head?
IF DOESN'T UNDERSTAND QUESTION:
Does someone or some force reach into your head and steal or remove your thoughts?

IF YES TO EITHER QUESTION:
Tell me about it.

THOUGHT INSERTION

Are there ever thoughts in your head that have been put in there from the outside?
IF YES: Tell me about it.
(I'm not referring to talking to someone who makes a suggestion or gives you advice. Instead I'm referring to thoughts getting inserted into your head from the outside. Does this ever happen?)

DELUSION OF GUILT

(Also see major depression section, page 36)
Do you think you've done something terrible and deserve to be punished?
IF YES: I know it will be hard to talk about, but what do you feel so guilty about?

Do you blame yourself for bad things going on in the world like wars, crime, starvation, etc.?

DELUSION OF GRANDIOSITY

(See Mania section, page 31)

DELUSION OF CONTROL

Do you ever get the feeling that you're being controlled by some force or power from the outside?
> **IF YES:** What's that like?
>> At times, does it seem like you're not in control of your body, almost like you're a puppet and something from the outside pulls the strings?
>>> **IF YES:** So, at times your body does certain things without your willing it?
>>>> **IF YES:** If I asked you to raise your hand or stand up now would you be able to do it?
>>>>> **IF NO:** Why is that?
>>>>> **IF YES:** So, you're in control of your actions? Are you always in control?

SOMATIC DELUSION

Are you concerned that you have a serious physical illness that a doctor hasn't found, or that something is wrong with your body?
> **IF YES:** What do you think is wrong?
>> Why do you think that?
>> Are you sure?

```
* * * * * * * * * * * * * *
```
HALLUCINATIONS
```
* * * * * * * * * * * * * *
```

VISUAL HALLUCINATIONS

Have you seen visions or other things that other people didn't see?
> **IF YES:** What did you see?
>> What time of the day did this occur?
>> How long ago did it start?
>> Do you see it every day?
>> How often do you see it?

AUDITORY HALLUCINATIONS

Have you heard noises, or sounds, or voices that other people didn't hear?
> **IF YES:** What did you hear?
> > Do the voices seem to come from inside or outside your head? **IF INSIDE:** But you hear it with your ears?
> > How many voices do you hear?
> > Are they male or female? Do you recognize them?
> > Do you ever hear two or more voices talking to each other?
> > Do the voices ever talk about what you're doing or thinking?
> > > **IF YES:** Do they ever keep up a running commentary on what you're doing or thinking just like a sports announcer describes a ballgame?
> > How long ago did the voices start?
> > Do you hear them every day?
> > How often during the day do you hear them?
> > Do they influence your behavior?
> > Do they tell you to do things?

TACTILE HALLUCINATIONS

Do you ever notice strange sensations in your body or on your skin?

Do you ever feel something creeping or crawling on your body, or something push or punch you but no one is there?
> **IF YES:** Like what?
> > When did it happen the first time?
> > How often has it happened?

OLFACTORY AND GUSTATORY HALLUCINATIONS

What about smells that other people don't notice, or strange tastes in your mouth?
> **IF YES:** Like what?
> > When did it happen the first time?
> > How often has it happened?
> > Are they associated with any other physical symptoms like an upset stomach, numbness, tingling, or brief memory loss?
> > > **IF YES:** Tell me about that.

MANIA/HYPOMANIA

Inclusion:* A, at least 3 or 4 from B, C
Exclusion: D, E

*Diagnostic Note: 1) In diagnosing mania and hypomania at least 3 items are required from B if the predominant mood is euphoric, at least 4 items are required if the predominant mood is irritable.

(A) MANIA: A distinct period of abnormally and persistently elevated, expansive, or irritable mood, lasting at least one week (or any duration if hospitalization is necessary).

(A) HYPOMANIA: A distinct period of persistently elevated, expansive, or irritable mood, lasting throughout at least four days, that is clearly different from the usual nondepressed mood.

Have there been times lasting at least a few days when you felt the opposite of depressed, that is when you were very cheerful or high and this felt different than your normal self?

IF YES OR UNCLEAR:

Did you feel hyper, or like you were high on drugs, even though you hadn't taken anything?

Did anything cause your good mood?

How long did it last?

So, was this more than just feeling good?

When did this occur?

How many periods like this have you had?

IF NO: What about a period lasting at least a few days when you were unusually irritable, and quick to argue or fight?

IF YES: Describe what that was like.

Were you using drugs or alcohol?

Did you get into many arguments or fights?

How long did this period last?

Was there a reason you felt that way?

When did it occur?

How many periods like this have you had?

Now I'm going to ask about some other things that you might have been thinking or feeling when you were feeling [HIGH, HYPER, EUPHORIC, IRRITABLE, etc.]...

B. **During the period of mood disturbance, at least three of the following have persisted (four if the mood is only irritable) and have been present to a significant degree:**

(B1) Inflated self-esteem or grandiosity.

What was your self-esteem like during this time?

Did you feel more self-confident than usual?

Did you think you had special talents, abilities, or powers?
   IF YES: Like what?

When some people feel [HIGH, EUPHORIC, etc.] they may think they're going to become famous or do great things. Did you have any thoughts like that? **IF YES:** Like what?

(B2) Decreased need for sleep (e.g., feels rested after only three hours of sleep).

During this time, how did you sleep?

Did you need less sleep than usual in order to feel rested?

(B3) More talkative than usual or pressure to keep talking.

Were you more talkative than usual?

Did you talk on and on so that people couldn't shut you up or interrupt?

Did you feel a pressure to talk constantly?

Did you talk faster than normal?
   IF YES: Did you talk so fast that people couldn't understand you?

(B4) Flight of ideas or subjective experience that thoughts are racing.

During this time, did it feel like your thoughts were going very fast and racing through your mind?

(B5) Distractibility (i.e., attention too easily drawn to unimportant or irrelevant external stimuli).

Were you easily distracted so that any little thing could get you off track? **IF YES:** What was that like?

(B6) Increase in goal-directed activity (either socially, at work or school, or sexually) or psychomotor agitation.

Were you more active than usual? For example, did you do more chores around the house?

Were you so energetic that instead of sleeping you did household chores or work throughout the night?

Did you start new projects or take on added responsibilities?

Did you work more?

Did you call friends more?

Were you sexually more active than usual?

Did you feel physically restless so that it was hard to sit still and you were always moving or pacing back and forth?
  IF YES TO ANY OF ABOVE: Tell me what you did.

(B7) Excessive involvement in pleasurable activities that have a high potential for painful consequences (e.g., engaging in unrestrained buying sprees, sexual indiscretions, or foolish business investments).

Did you do anything that could have caused problems for you or your family? For example, when some people feel [MANIC MOOD] they go on spending sprees, write bad checks, invest money foolishly, or do things sexually that are unusual for them. Did you do anything like that? **IF YES:** Like what?

(C) <u>MANIA:</u> The mood disturbance is sufficiently severe to cause marked impairment in occupational functioning or in usual social activities or relationships with others, or to necessitate hospitalization to prevent harm to self or others, or there are psychotic features.

(C) **HYPOMANIA:** The episode is associated with an unequivocal change in functioning that is uncharacteristic of the person when not symptomatic, and the disturbance in mood and change in functioning is observable by others.

Did anyone notice that there was something different about you?
   IF YES: What did they say?
   IF NO: Did anyone notice [MANIA SYMPTOMS NOTED ABOVE]?

What effect did this episode have on your life at the time it was going on?

Did it cause major problems in your job (school)?....marriage? ....relationships with friends or family?....social life?
   IF YES TO ANY ITEM: What happened?

Did anyone notice that you weren't functioning the way you normally do?
   IF YES: What did they say?

Did you get treatment?
   IF YES: Were you hospitalized?

(D) **Exclude** the diagnosis if during the course of the illness the patient had delusions or hallucinations for at least two weeks in the absence of prominent mood symptoms. In such cases the diagnosis is schizophrenia, schizoaffective disorder, delusional disorder, schizophreniform disorder, or psychotic disorder NOS.

(See pages 26-29 for psychosis questions.)
IF PSYCHOTIC:
   Was there a time when you [PSYCHOTIC SYMPTOM] but did not feel [MANIC MOOD] and have problems with [MANIC SYMPTOMS]?
      IF YES: How long did you have [PSYCHOTIC SYMPTOMS] only?
      When did the [MANIC MOOD AND SYMPTOMS] begin in relation to this?

(E) **Exclude** the diagnosis if the symptoms are due to physical illness (e.g., hyperthyroidism), or street drugs (amphetamines, cocaine).

MAJOR DEPRESSION

Inclusion: A1 or A2, at least 5 from A, B
Exclusion: C-E

NOTE: For each symptom you must inquire about duration (For how long have you...) and persistence (Do you feel like that nearly every day?).

NOTE: Do not include symptoms that are clearly due to a physical illness, or mood incongruent delusions or hallucinations.

A. At least five of the following symptoms have been present during the same two week period and represent a change from previous functioning; at least one symptom is either 1) depressed mood or 2) loss of interest or pleasure.

(A1) Depressed mood most of the day, nearly every day, as indicated by either subjective report (e.g., feels sad or empty) or observation made by others (e.g., appears tearful).

How is your mood?
Have you been feeling sad, blue, down, or depressed?
  IF YES: For how long have you been feeling [DEPRESSED, DOWN, etc]?
          Do you feel that way nearly every day?
          How much of the day does it last?
          How bad is the feeling?

(A2) Markedly diminished interest or pleasure in all, or almost all, activities most of the day, nearly every day.

Have you lost interest in or do you get less pleasure from the things you used to enjoy?
  IF YES: What do you normally enjoy doing? (Television? Reading? Sports? Shopping? Socializing? Eating? Hobbies? Sex?)
          What do you still enjoy?
          What have you lost interest in?
          For how long have you not enjoyed these things like you used to?
          Is it like that nearly every day?

(A3) **Significant weight loss when not dieting or weight gain (e.g., a change of more than 5% of body weight in a month), or decrease or increase in appetite nearly every day.**

Has there been any change in your appetite?
IF INCREASED OR DECREASED:
How much more/less have you been eating?
Is it like that nearly every day?
For how long has your appetite been increased/decreased?

Have you gained/lost any weight? **IF YES:** How much? Since when?

(A4) **Insomnia or hypersomnia nearly every day.**

How have you been sleeping?
How many hours per night have you been sleeping?
How does this compare to normal?
IF INCREASED OR DECREASED:
Is it a problem nearly every day?
For how long have you had sleep problems?
IF DECREASED: Do you have problems falling asleep, staying asleep, or waking up too early in the morning?

(A5) **Psychomotor agitation or retardation nearly every day (observable by others, not merely subjective feelings of restlessness or being slowed down).**

<u>Observation</u> of psychomotor agitation (fidgety while sitting; pacing; pulling on hair, skin, or clothing; handwringing; crossing and uncrossing legs frequently) and/or psychomotor retardation (slowed speech; long pauses before answering questions or between words; mute; slowed body movements) by interviewer or others.

Agitation: Have you been more fidgety and having problems sitting still?
IF YES: Do you pace back and forth?
Have others noticed your restlessness?

Retardation: Have you felt slowed down, like you were moving in slow motion or stuck in mud?
IF YES: Have others noticed this?

(A6) Fatigue or loss of energy nearly every day.

How has your energy level been?
Have you been feeling tired or worn out?
  IF YES: Duration and persistence questions. (See top of pg. 34)

(A7) Feelings of worthlessness or excessive or inappropriate guilt nearly every day (not merely self-reproach or guilt about being sick).

How have you been feeling about yourself?
What's your self-esteem been like?
  IF LOW: What type of thoughts do you have about yourself?
              Do you feel like you're worthless or a failure?
                IF YES: Tell me about it.

Have you been blaming yourself for things?
  IF YES: Like what?

Do you feel guilty?
  IF YES: About what?
              How hard is it to get your mind off of this?
              Do you think about things from the past and feel guilty
              about them?
                IF YES: Like what?

  IF EVIDENCE OF GUILT OR WORTHLESSNESS:
  How often do you actually think [PATIENT'S DESCRIPTION OF
  GUILT OR WORTHLESSNESS]? (Is it on your mind every day?)

(A8) Diminished ability to think or concentrate, or indecisiveness, nearly every day.

Have you been having problems thinking or concentrating?
  IF YES: What does this interfere with?
              Are you able to read?   Watch TV?   Follow a
              conversation?
              Duration and persistence questions.

Is it harder to make decisions than before?
  IF YES: What kind of decisions are harder to make?
              (What about every day decisions?)
              Duration and persistence questions.

(A9) **Recurrent thoughts of death (not just fear of dying), recurrent suicidal ideation without a specific plan, or a suicide attempt or a specific plan for committing suicide.**

Sometimes when a person feels down or depressed they might think about dying. Have you been having any thoughts like that?
　　IF YES: Tell me about it. Have you thought about taking your life?
　　　　　　　IF YES: Did you think of a way to do it?
　　　　　　　　　　　　How close have you come to doing it?
　　　　　　　IF NO: Do you wish you were dead?
　　　　　　　　　　　　When you go to sleep, do you often wish you would not wake up?

(B) **The symptoms cause clinically significant distress or impairment in social, occupational, or other important areas of functioning.**

What difficulties in your life has the depression caused?
Does it bother you a lot that you feel this way?
Has it caused problems in your job (school)?....marriage? ....relationships with friends or family?....social life?....doing household chores?

(C) **Exclude the diagnosis if the symptoms are due to physical illness (endocrine disorder), medication (antihypertensives), or street drugs (alcohol, cocaine withdrawal, PCP, steroids).**

(D) **Exclude the diagnosis if the depression occurs within two months of the loss of a loved one (except if associated with marked functional impairment, morbid preoccupation with worthlessness, suicidal ideation, psychotic symptoms, or psychomotor retardation).**

(E) **Exclude the diagnosis if during the course of the illness the patient had delusions or hallucinations for at least two weeks in the absence of prominent mood symptoms. In such cases the diagnosis is schizophrenia, schizoaffective disorder, delusional disorder, schizophreniform disorder, or psychotic disorder NOS.**

(See pages 26-29 for psychosis questions.)
IF PSYCHOTIC:
　　Was there a time when you [PSYCHOTIC SX] but did not feel sad or depressed and have problems with [DEPRESSIVE SX]?
　　　　IF YES: How long did you have [PSYCHOTIC SXS] only?
　　　　　　　　　When did the depression begin in relation to this?

DYSTHYMIC DISORDER

Inclusion: A, at least 2 from B, C, H
Exclusion: D-G

(A) **Depressed mood for most of the day, for more days than not, as indicated either by subjective account or observation of others, for at least two years.**

How is your mood?
Have you been feeling sad, blue, down, or depressed?
    IF YES: How often? (On more days than not?)
              For how long have you felt this way?
              (Has it been at least two years?)

Diagnostic Note: To diagnose dysthymia you must ensure that major depression has not been present during the past two years.

Recently, have you been more severely depressed than usual?
    IF NO: Was there a time in the past two years lasting at least two weeks when you felt more severely depressed than usual?
                IF YES TO EITHER: See pages 34-37 for major depression questions.

IF CURRENT MAJOR DEPRESSION:
For how long have you been feeling severely depressed with symptoms like [CURRENT DEPRESSIVE SYMPTOMS]? Before that, were you still bothered by a low level of depression?
    IF YES: Was that low level of depression present on most days?
                IF YES: So, even before this current episode of more severe depression, you were bothered by a milder depression on most days. Right?
                          For how long did you have the milder depression?

IF MAJOR DEPRESSION DURING PAST TWO YEARS:
Since you improved from your serious depression occurring last [DATE], have you still felt sad, blue, or depressed on most days?
    IF YES: Is that how you were before you got more severely depressed?
                IF YES: For how long before the serious depression were you bothered by the milder depression?

(B)   Presence, while depressed, of at least two of the following:

During this time (the time of the low level depression), do you often...
1) ...have a poor appetite or overeat?
2) ...have difficulty sleeping or with oversleeping?
3) ...feel tired?
4) ...feel down on yourself, or have low self-esteem?
5) ...have problems concentrating or making decisions?
6) ...feel hopeless or pessimistic about the future?

(C)   During the two year period of the disturbance, never without the symptoms in A and B for more than two months at a time.

During the [DYSTHYMIA TIME PERIOD] were you ever free of depression or sadness for a couple of months or more? Were you ever free of [SYMPTOMS IN B] for a couple of months or more?

(D)   <u>Exclude</u> the diagnosis if a major depression occurred during the first two years of the dysthymia.

When did the low level depression begin? See pages 34-37 for major depression questions, and determine if major depressive episode occurred during first two years of onset of dysthymia.

(E)   <u>Exclude</u> the diagnosis if the individual has a history of a manic or hypomanic episode.

(F)   <u>Exclude</u> diagnosis if the symptoms are superimposed on a chronic psychotic disorder such as schizophrenia or delusional disorder.

(G)   <u>Exclude</u> the diagnosis if the symptoms are due to the direct physiological effects of a substance (e.g., a drug of abuse, medication), or a general medical condition (e.g., hypothyroidism).

(H)   The symptoms cause clinically significant distress or impairment in social, occupational, or other important areas of functioning.

What difficulties in your life has the low level depression caused?
Does it bother you a lot that you feel this way?
Has it caused problems in your job (school)?....marriage?
....relationships with friends or family?....social life?....doing household chores?

PANIC DISORDER

> Inclusion: A
> Exclusion: B, C

Diagnostic Note: Panic disorder can be diagnosed with or without agoraphobia. See pages 42-43 for agoraphobia questions.

(A) Recurrent unexpected panic attacks (see criteria for a panic attack on page 41), at least one of which has been followed by at least a month of one of the following: 1) persistent concern about having additional attacks, 2) worry about the implications of the attack or its consequences (e.g., losing control, having a heart attack, "going crazy"), or 3) a significant change in behavior related to the attacks.

An anxiety or panic attack is a sudden rush of intense fear, anxiety, or discomfort that comes on from out of the blue for no apparent reason, or in situations where you did not expect it to occur. Have you ever experienced this?
>   IF YES: What was it like? (Ask about symptoms specified on page 41.)
>   How many attacks have you experienced?
>   Do they ever awaken you from sleep?
>   Does anything bring them on?
>   **IF SPECIFIC SITUATION DESCRIBED:**
>   Do they only occur in these situations, or have these attacks also sometimes come on from out of the blue, or in situations where you did not expect them?

Do you worry a lot about having more of them?
>   IF YES: How long would it take before you would stop worrying that another attack would occur?

What are you afraid might happen from these anxiety attacks? (Do you worry a lot that you might have a heart attack? Are you often worried that you might go crazy or lose control?)
>   IF YES: For how long have you worried about that?

Have you changed your behavior or routine since these attacks began?

A panic attack refers to a discrete period of intense fear or discomfort, in which at least four of the following symptoms developed abruptly and reached a peak within 10 minutes.

Think of the last bad attack you had. When was it? Where were you at the time? I'm going to ask you about some symptoms you may have experienced during that attack. Did you...

1) ...feel your heart racing, pounding, fluttering, or skipping beats?
2) ...sweat?
3) ...tremble or shake?
4) ...have trouble catching your breath, or feel like you were being smothered?
5) ...feel like you were choking?
6) ...have chest pain, pressure, tightness, or discomfort?
7) ...feel nauseated, sick to your stomach, or like you might have diarrhea?
8) ...feel dizzy, light-headed, unsteady, or like you might faint?
9) ...feel like things around you were unreal, like you were in a dream, like parts of your body were unreal or detached from you, or like you were outside of yourself, watching?
10) ...fear you were going crazy or might lose control?
11) ...fear you might die?
12) ...feel numb or tingling in your fingers or feet?
13) ...have hot flashes or chills?

During a bad attack, how long does it usually take from the time it begins until you have most of the symptoms like [SYMPTOMS NOTED ABOVE]?
(IF UNCLEAR OR GREATER THAN TEN MINUTES):
Would most of the symptoms ever come on quickly, within ten minutes after the attack began?

(B)   Exclude the diagnosis if the symptoms are due to the direct physiological effects of a substance (e.g., a drug of abuse, a medication) or a general medical condition (e.g., hyperthyroidism).

(C)   Exclude the diagnosis if the anxiety is better accounted for by another mental disorder, such as obsessive-compulsive disorder, posttraumatic stress disorder, separation anxiety disorder, specific phobia, or social phobia.

AGORAPHOBIA

> Inclusion: A, B
> Exclusion: C

Diagnostic Note: Agoraphobia can be diagnosed with or without a history of panic disorder. See pages 40-41 for panic disorder questions.

(A) Anxiety about being in places or situations from which escape might be difficult (or embarrassing) or in which help might not be available in the event of having an unexpected or situationally predisposed panic attack or panic-like symptoms. Agoraphobic fears typically involve characteristic clusters of situations that include being outside the home alone; being in a crowd or standing in a line; being on a bridge; and traveling in a bus, train, or car. NOTE: Consider the diagnosis of specific phobia if the avoidance is limited to one or only a few specific situations, or social phobia if the avoidance is limited to social situations.

Some people have very strong fears of being in certain places or in certain situations. Do any of the following make you feel very fearful, anxious, or nervous?

   a) Being away from home alone.
   b) Being in crowded places like a movie theater, supermarket, shopping mall, church, restaurant, etc.
   c) Standing in long lines.
   d) Being on a bridge or in a tunnel.
   e) Traveling in a bus, train, or plane.
   f) Driving or riding in a car.
   g) Being home alone.
   h) Being in wide open spaces like a park.
   i) Being in a closed in space (e.g., small rooms, elevators)
       IF YES TO ANY OF ABOVE:
           I know it may be difficult to describe, but what is it about [PHOBIA] that worries you?
           What do you think might happen to you?
           What are you afraid of?

(B)   **The situations are avoided (e.g., travel is restricted), or else endured
with marked distress or with anxiety about having a panic attack or
panic-like symptoms, or require the presence of a companion.**

To what degree do you avoid [PHOBIA]?
   IF NO AVOIDANCE:
      So what do you do, how do you cope?
      Does having someone with you help?
      Do you [PHOBIA] only when you're with someone?
      Do you [PHOBIA] alone?
         IF YES: How bad does the anxiety get?
                        What are you anxious about?

(C)   <u>Exclude</u> the diagnosis if the anxiety or phobic avoidance is better
accounted for by another mental disorder, such as obsessive-
compulsive disorder (e.g., avoidance of contamination); posttraumatic stress disorder (e.g., avoidance of stimuli associated with
a severe stressor); separation anxiety disorder (e.g., avoidance of
leaving parents); social phobia (e.g., avoidance limited to social
situations because of fear of embarrassment); or specific phobia
(e.g., avoidance limited to a single situation like elevators).

SOCIAL PHOBIA

> Inclusion: A-E
> Exclusion: F, G

(A) A marked and persistent fear of one or more social or performance situations in which the person is exposed to unfamiliar people or to possible scrutiny by others. The individual fears that he or she will act in a way (or show anxiety symptoms) that will be humiliating or embarrassing.

Some people have very strong fears of being watched or evaluated by others. Do you worry that you might do or say something that would embarrass you in front of others, or that other people might think badly of you?

Let me ask about some specific situations. Do any of the following make you feel more fearful, anxious, or nervous than most people?

    a) Eating in front of others.
    b) Writing in front of others.
    c) Public speaking.
    d) Saying something when in a group of people.
    e) Asking a question when in a group of people.
    f) Urinating in public restrooms.
    g) Business meetings.
    h) Parties.
        IF YES TO ANY: Do you think you are much more anxious than other people?

I know it may be difficult to describe, but what is it about [PHOBIA] that worries you (e.g., choking when eating; hand trembling with writing; being unable to urinate; not being able to complete a lecture, speech, or presentation)?

(B) Exposure to the feared social situation almost invariably provokes anxiety, which may take the form of a situationally bound or situationally predisposed panic attack.

Whenever you [PHOBIA] do you immediately get anxious or nervous?

    IF YES: What is that like?

           Do you have a panic attack?

    IF NO, OR THERE IS COMPLETE AVOIDANCE OF PHOBIC STIMULUS: What about in the past?

(C)   **The person recognizes that the fear is excessive or unreasonable.**

Do you think you are more afraid and worried about [PHOBIA] than
you should be?
>   **IF NO:**   You <u>really</u> don't believe that you worry too much about
>   [PHOBIA]?
>>   **IF NO:**   Then why do you think other people aren't as
>>   concerned about/worried by [PHOBIA]?

(D)   **The feared social or performance situations are avoided, or else
endured with intense anxiety or distress.**

To what degree to you avoid [PHOBIA]?
>   **IF NO AVOIDANCE:**   How bad does the anxiety get when you
>   [PHOBIA]? Do you have a panic attack?

(E)   **The avoidance, anxious anticipation, or distress in the feared social
or performance situation(s) interferes significantly with the person's
normal routine, occupational (academic) functioning, or social
activities or relationships, or there is marked distress about having
the phobia.**

What problems in your life has the avoidance/fear of [PHOBIA]
caused?
Has it caused job (or school) problems like getting fired or failure
to get promoted?
What about marital problems?
What about interfering with friendships?
What about affecting leisure time activities?
How much does it bother you that you have this fear of [PHOBIA]?

(F)   <u>Exclude</u> **the diagnosis if the fear or avoidance is due to the direct
physiological effects of a substance (e.g., drugs of abuse,
medication) or a general medical condition, or is better accounted for
by panic disorder with or without agoraphobia, specific phobia,
separation anxiety disorder, body dysmorphic disorder, a pervasive
developmental disorder, or schizoid personality disorder.**

(G)   <u>Exclude</u> **the diagnosis if the fear is related to another psychiatric or
physical disorder (e.g., fear of a panic attack, stuttering, Parkinsonian
trembling, anorexic or bulimic abnormal eating behavior).**

SPECIFIC PHOBIA (SIMPLE PHOBIA)

> Inclusion: A-E
> Exclusion: F

(A) **Marked and persistent fear that is excessive or unreasonable, cued by the presence or anticipation of a specific object or situation (e.g., flying, heights, animals, receiving an injection, seeing blood).**

Some people have very strong fears of certain objects or situations. Do any of the following make you feel very fearful or nervous?

   a) Heights
   b) Being near household pets like cats or dogs
   c) Spiders, bugs, snakes, mice, or bats
   d) Flying
   e) Seeing blood
   f) Being in water (e.g., swimming pools, lakes)
   g) Storms
   h) Receiving an injection
      IF YES TO ANY: Do you think you are more anxious than other people?

NOTE: Do not include fears related to agoraphobia or social phobia.

(B) **Exposure to the phobic stimulus almost invariably provokes an immediate anxiety response, which may take the form of a situationally bound or situationally predisposed panic attack.**

Whenever you [PHOBIA] do you immediately get anxious or nervous?
   IF YES: What is that like?
         Do you have a panic attack?
   IF NO, OR THERE IS COMPLETE AVOIDANCE OF PHOBIC STIMULUS: What about in the past?

(C) **The person recognizes that the fear is excessive or unreasonable.**

Do you think you are more afraid and worried about [PHOBIA] than you should be?
   IF NO: You <u>really</u> don't believe that you worry too much about [PHOBIA]?
         IF NO: Then, why do you think other people aren't as concerned about/worried by [PHOBIA]?

(D) **The phobic situation(s) is avoided, or else endured with intense anxiety or distress.**

To what degree do you avoid [PHOBIA]?
IF NO AVOIDANCE:
How bad does the anxiety get when you [PHOBIA]?
How upset do you get when you [PHOBIA]?

(E) **The avoidance, anxious anticipation, or distress in the feared situation(s) interferes significantly with the person's normal routine, occupational (academic) functioning, or social activities or relationships, or there is marked distress about having the phobia.**

What problems in your life has the avoidance/fear of [PHOBIA] caused? Has it interfered with your routine?
What about job (or school) problems?
What about marital problems?
What about interfering with friendships?
What about affecting leisure time activities (e.g., outings, vacations)?
How much does it bother you that you have this fear of [PHOBIA]?

(F) <u>Exclude</u> **the diagnosis if the anxiety, panic attacks, or phobic avoidance associated with the specific object or situation are better accounted for by another mental disorder, such as obsessive-compulsive disorder (e.g., fear of contamination); posttraumatic stress disorder (e.g., avoidance of stimuli associated with a severe stressor); separation anxiety disorder (e.g., avoidance of school); social phobia (e.g., avoidance of social situations because of fear of embarrassment); panic disorder, or agoraphobia.**

GENERALIZED ANXIETY DISORDER

Inclusion: A, B, at least 3 from C, E
Exclusion: D, F

(A) Excessive anxiety and worry (apprehensive expectation), occurring more days than not for at least six months, about a number of events or activities (such as work or school performance).

During the past several months, have you frequently been worried or anxious about a number of things in your daily life?
   IF YES: What have you worried about?
           Do people say you worry about these things too much? Do you think you do?
           Do you think your anxiety is unrealistic or excessive?
           Do you worry that something bad is going to happen to you, or to someone close to you?
           How often do you worry about these things? (On more days than not?)
           For how long? (Has it been at least six months?)

(B) The person finds it difficult to control the worry.

Is it hard for you to control or stop your worrying?

(C) The anxiety and worry are associated with at least three of the following six symptoms (with at least some symptoms present for more days than not for the past six months).

Now I'm going to ask you about physical symptoms that often go along with anxiety and nervousness. During the past 6 months, when you are feeling nervous or tense, do you often...

   1) ...feel restless, fidgety, jittery, keyed up, on edge, or have difficulty sitting still?
   2) ...get tired very easily?
   3) ...have problems concentrating, or does your "mind go blank?"
   4) ...feel irritable?
   5) ...feel tension, aches, or soreness in your muscles?
   6) ...have problems falling asleep or staying asleep?

How often do you have these physical symptoms? (On more days than not?)

(D) <u>Exclude</u> the diagnosis if the focus of the anxiety and worry are confined to experiencing features of another Axis I disorder, such as anxiety or worry about having a panic attack (as in panic disorder), being embarrassed in public (as in social phobia), being contaminated (as in obsessive-compulsive disorder), gaining weight (as in anorexia nervosa), having multiple physical complaints (as in somatization disorder), or having a serious illness (as in hypochondriasis), and the anxiety and worry do not occur exclusively during posttraumatic stress disorder.

(E) The anxiety, worry, or physical symptoms cause clinically significant distress or impairment in social, occupational, or other important areas of functioning.

What effect has the anxiety, worry, and [SYMPTOMS FROM C] had on your life?
Does it bother you a lot that you feel this way?
Has it affected your job (school)?....marriage?.... relationship with friends?....social life?...leisure activities?
  IF YES: In what way?

Does it interfere with or keep you from completing your daily routine and chores?

(F) <u>Exclude</u> the diagnosis if the symptoms are due to the direct effects of a substance (e.g., a drug of abuse, a medication) or a general medical condition (e.g., hyperthyroidism), or are present only during the course of a mood disorder, a psychotic disorder, or a pervasive developmental disorder.

POSTTRAUMATIC STRESS DISORDER

Inclusion: A1, A2, at least 1 from B, 3 from C, 2 from D, E, F
Exclusion: None

(A1) **The person has been exposed to a traumatic event in which he/she experienced, witnessed, or was confronted with an event or events that involved actual or threatened death or serious injury, or a threat to the physical integrity of oneself or others.**

Have you ever seen or experienced a traumatic event in which your life was actually in danger, or you thought your life was in danger?
   IF YES: What happened?

Have you ever witnessed an event in which someone else's life seemed to be in danger?
   IF YES: What happened?

What about traumatic events in which you or someone else were seriously injured, or could have been seriously injured?
   IF YES: What happened?

(A2) **The person's response to the traumatic event involved intense fear, helplessness, or horror.**

How did you react when you [TRAUMA]?
(Were you frightened or horrified?)
(Did you feel helpless and out of control?)

B. **The traumatic event is persistently reexperienced in at least one of the following ways:**

(B1) **Recurrent and intrusive distressing recollections of the event, including images, thoughts, or perceptions.**

Do memories about the [TRAUMA] still bother you?
Do you see images of the trauma?
   IF YES TO EITHER: Tell me about them. How frequent are they? Do you try to put them out of you head, but sometimes can't?

(B2) **Recurrent distressing dreams of the event.**

What about dreams of the [TRAUMA]? (Describe)

(B3) Acting or feeling as if the traumatic event were recurring (includes a sense of reliving the experience, illusions, hallucinations, and dissociative flashback episodes, including those that occur on awakening or when intoxicated).

Some people who experience such terrible events sometimes have flashbacks where they relive the event, and they may even act or feel as though the event is happening again, even though it isn't. Has this happened to you?
   IF YES: Describe.
   IF NO: Have you ever had hallucinations of the episode? (Have you heard voices or seen visions from the [TRAUMA])?

(B4) Intense psychological distress at exposure to internal or external cues that symbolize or resemble an aspect of the traumatic event.

Are there things that remind you of the [TRAUMA] that get you upset?
   IF YES: Describe.
   IF NO: Do you feel bad on the anniversary of the [TRAUMA]?

(B5) Physiological reactivity upon exposure to internal or external cues that symbolize or resemble an aspect of the traumatic event.

Do reminders of the [TRAUMA] make you tremble, break out into a sweat, hyperventilate, or have a racing heart?

C. Persistent avoidance of stimuli associated with the trauma and numbing of general responsiveness (not present before the trauma), as indicated by at least three of the following:

(C1) Efforts to avoid thoughts, feelings, or conversations associated with the trauma.

Do you try to block out thoughts or feelings related to the [TRAUMA]? Do you avoid talking about it?

(C2) Efforts to avoid activities, places, or people that arouse recollections of the trauma.

Do you try to avoid activities, situations, or places that remind you of the [TRAUMA]? **IF YES:** Like what?
Do you avoid people who remind you of it?

(C3) Inability to recall an important aspect of the trauma.

Are there some aspects of the [TRAUMA] that you can't recall?
   IF YES: Like what?

(C4) Markedly diminished interest or participation in significant activities.

Have you noticed that since the [TRAUMA] you've lost interest in
some things you used to enjoy? **IF YES:** Like what?

Are there any activities you no longer participate in since it
occurred? **IF YES:** Like what?

(C5) Feeling of detachment or estrangement from others.

Do you frequently feel like you don't fit in with the people around
you? That is, you're with them physically, but you feel distant and
cutoff from them.

(C6) Restricted range of affect (e.g., unable to have loving feelings).

Does it seem like you've lost the ability to feel certain emotions?
   IF YES: Like what?
Do you feel emotionally numb?
(Has it seemed like you no longer experience strong feelings about
anything, or that you can't feel love anymore?)

**(C7) Sense of a foreshortened future (e.g., does not expect to have a
career, marriage, children, or a normal life span).**

Has the [TRAUMA] changed how you feel about the future?

Have you given up on some goals that you used to have for
yourself? **IF YES:** Like what?

After a traumatic event some people feel different about things
they've always wanted such as a career, marriage, having kids,
living a long life. Did the trauma affect you in any way like this?
   IF YES: In what way?

D. **Persistent symptoms of increased arousal (not present before the trauma), as indicated by at least two of the following:**

(D3) Difficulty falling or staying asleep.

Since the [TRAUMA] have you had problems sleeping?

(D2) Irritability or outbursts of anger.

Have you been more irritable or lost your temper more easily?

(D3) Difficulty concentrating.

Since the [TRAUMA] have you had problems concentrating?
  IF YES: In what areas?

(D4) Hypervigilance.

Since the [TRAUMA] have you been on the alert, always keeping your guard up with an eye out for possible trouble?

(D5) Exaggerated startle response.

Have you been kind of jumpy and easily startled by everyday, ordinary noises and movement?

(E) **Duration of the disturbance (symptoms in Criteria B, C, and D) is more than one month.**

For how long have you been bothered by (SYMPTOMS IN B-D)?

(F) **The disturbance causes clinically significant distress or impairment in social, occupational, or other important areas of functioning.**

What effect has this trauma had on your life?

Do you often feel extremely upset or distressed because of it?

Has it affected your job (school)?....marriage?....relationship with friends?....social life?...leisure activities? **IF YES:** In what way?

Has it interfered with or kept you from completing your daily routine and chores?

ACUTE STRESS DISORDER

> Inclusion: A1, A2, at least 3 from B, C-G
> Exclusion: H

(A1) The person has been exposed to a traumatic event in which he/she experienced, witnessed, or was confronted with an event or events that involved actual or threatened death or serious injury, or a threat to the physical integrity of oneself or others.

Have you ever seen or experienced a traumatic event in which your life was actually in danger, or you thought your life was in danger?
    IF YES: What happened?

Have you ever witnessed an event in which someone else's life seemed to be in danger?
    IF YES: What happened?

What about traumatic events in which you or someone else were seriously injured, or could have been seriously injured?
    IF YES: What happened?

(A2) The person's response to the traumatic event involved intense fear, helplessness, or horror.

How did you react when you [TRAUMA]?
(Were you frightened or horrified?)
(Did you feel helpless and out of control?)

B.   Either while experiencing or after experiencing the distressing event, the individual has at least three of the following dissociative symptoms:

(B1) A subjective sense of numbing, detachment, or absence of emotional responsiveness.

What was your emotional reaction while it was happening?
What about after it happened?

Either while the [TRAUMA] happened, or afterwards, did you feel emotionally numb, or distant and cutoff from people?

(B2) A reduction in awareness of his or her surrounding (e.g., "being in a daze").

Did you feel like you were "in a daze?"

Did it seem like you were less aware of everything else going on around you?

(B3) Derealization.

While it was happening, or afterwards, did it seem like things were unreal, or like everything was a dream?
Did things around you seem somehow strange, or changed in shape or size?
  IF YES TO EITHER: Describe what that was like.

(B4) Depersonalization.

Did it seem like your body or some part of your body was somehow changed, not real, or detached from you?

Did you feel like you were watching yourself from outside your body?

(B5) Dissociative amnesia (i.e., inability to recall an important aspect of the trauma).

After the [TRAUMA] did you have a brief blackout, and forget some important aspect of the event?

(C) The traumatic event is persistently reexperienced in at least one of the following ways: recurrent images, thoughts, dreams, illusions, flashback episodes, or a sense of reliving the experience; or distress on exposure to reminders of the traumatic event.

Do memories about the [TRAUMA] still bother you?
Do you see images of the trauma?
  IF YES TO EITHER: Tell me about them. How frequent are they? Do you try to put them out of you head, but sometimes can't?

What about dreams of the [TRAUMA]? (Describe)

Some people who experience such terrible events sometimes have flashbacks where they relive the event. They may either act or feel as though the event is happening again, even though it isn't. Has this happened to you?
   IF YES: Describe.
   IF NO: Have you ever had hallucinations of the episode? (Have you heard voices or seen visions from the [TRAUMA])?

Are there things that remind you of the [TRAUMA] that get you upset?
   IF YES: Describe.
   IF NO: Do you feel bad on the anniversary of the [TRAUMA]?

Do reminders of the [TRAUMA] make you tremble, break out into a sweat, hyperventilate, or have a racing heart?

(D)   **Marked avoidance of stimuli that arouse recollections of the trauma (e.g., thoughts, feelings, conversations, activities, places or people).**

Do you try to block out thoughts or feelings related to the [TRAUMA]? Do you avoid talking about it?

Do you try to avoid activities, situations, or places that remind you of the [TRAUMA]? **IF YES:** Like what?

Do you avoid people who remind you of it?

(E)   **Marked symptoms of anxiety or increased arousal (e.g., difficulty sleeping, irritability, poor concentration, hypervigilance, exaggerated startle response, and motor restlessness).**

Since the [TRAUMA] have you had problems sleeping?

Have you been more irritable or lost your temper more easily?

Since the [TRAUMA] have you had problems concentrating?
   IF YES: In what areas?

Since the [TRAUMA] have you been on the alert, always keeping your guard up with an eye out for possible trouble?

Have you been kind of jumpy and easily startled by everyday, ordinary noises and movement?

Have you felt fidgety or restless?

(F) The disturbance causes clinically significant distress or impairment in social, occupational, or other important areas of functioning or impairs the individual's ability to pursue some necessary task, such as obtaining necessary assistance or mobilizing personal resources by telling family members about the traumatic experience.

What effect has this trauma had on your life?

Do you often feel extremely upset or distressed because of it?

Has it effected your job (school)?....marriage?....relationship with friends?....social life? **IF YES:** In what way?

Has it interfered with or kept you from completing your daily routine and chores?

Were you able to tell your family what happened?
   IF YES: How hard was it to go to them?

ASK FOLLOWING QUESTIONS IF APPROPRIATE AND NECESSARY:

Were you able to get the medical help you needed?
Did you go to the police?
   IF NO TO EITHER: What kept you from doing that?

(G) The disturbance lasts for a minimum of two days and a maximum of four weeks and occurs within four weeks of the traumatic event.

For how long have you been bothered by [SYMPTOMS IN B-E]?

How soon after the trauma happened did the symptoms like [SYMPTOMS IN B-E] begin?

(H) <u>Exclude</u> the diagnosis if the symptoms are due to the direct effects of a substance (e.g., a drug of abuse, a medication) or a general medical condition, are better accounted for by brief psychotic disorder, and are not merely an exacerbation of a preexisting Axis I or Axis II disorder.

OBSESSIVE-COMPULSIVE DISORDER

Inclusion:	A1-A4 for obsessions or
	A1-A2 for compulsions
	B and C for either
Exclusion:	D, E

A. <u>OBSESSIONS</u> - A1-A4 are all required

(A1) Recurrent and persistent thoughts, impulses, or images that are experienced, at some time during the disturbance, as intrusive and inappropriate and cause marked anxiety and distress.

Some people are bothered by recurrent thoughts or impulses that seem inappropriate or do not make sense, but they keep repeating over and over and are difficult to get out of your mind. (For example, intrusive, repeated thoughts that you might hurt or kill someone you love even though you didn't want to; that someone you love is hurt; that you will yell obscenities in public; that you are contaminated by germs or dirt; or that you just hit someone while driving.) Has anything like this been a problem for you?
> IF YES: Describe what it's like.
>
> How often does it happen?
>
> How do you feel when you have these thoughts?

What about intrusive, frequent, repeated images?
> IF YES: Tell me about it.
>
> How often does it happen?
>
> How do you feel when you have these images?

(A2) The thoughts, impulses, or images are not simply excessive worries about real-life problems.

(A3) The person attempts to ignore or suppress such thoughts, impulses, or images, or to neutralize them with some other thought or action.

What do you do to deal with this?

Do you try to ignore or get rid of these thoughts/images and put them out of your mind?

Do you tell yourself things or imagine certain other images in order to neutralize or counteract the unpleasant thought/image?

(A4) **The person recognizes that the obsessional thoughts, impulses, or images are a product of his or her own mind (not imposed from without as in thought insertion).**

Are these your own thoughts, or do you believe they are put into your head by someone, or some force or power from the outside?
   IF OUTSIDE: Tell me how that happens.

COMPULSIONS - A1 and A2 are both required

(A1) **Repetitive behaviors (e.g., hand washing, ordering, checking), or mental acts (e.g., praying, counting, repeating words silently) that the person feels driven to perform in response to an obsession, or according to rules that must be applied rigidly.**

Some people are bothered by having to do something over and over that they can't resist when they try. For example, they wash their hands repeatedly, check whether the door is locked or the stove is turned off, or count things excessively. Have you had any difficulties like this?
   IF YES: Like what?
         Describe what it's like.

Do you have any rituals that you always have to do in a particular order, and if the order is wrong you have to start all over from the beginning?   **IF YES:** Like what?

(A2) **The behaviors or mental acts are aimed at preventing or reducing distress or preventing some dreaded event or situation; however, these behaviors or mental acts either are not connected in a realistic way with what they are designed to neutralize or prevent or are clearly excessive.**

If you do not [COMPULSION], do you get very anxious or tense?
   IF NO: So, why do you do it?

What do you think might happen if you didn't [COMPULSION]?

Criteria B-E are the same for both obsessions and compulsions.

(B)   At some point during the course of the disorder, the person has recognized that the obsessions and compulsions are excessive or unreasonable.

Does the [OBSESSION/COMPULSION] seem unreasonable or excessive, but you still feel compelled to do it?
IF NO: Did you <u>ever</u> think the [OBSESSION/COMPULSION] was unreasonable or excessive?
IF NO: Did other people think so?
IF YES: What did they say?
Do you think they're wrong?

(C)   The obsessions or compulsions cause marked distress, are time-consuming (take more than an hour a day), or significantly interfere with the person's normal routine, occupational (or academic) functioning, or usual social activities or relationships.

Does it bother you a lot that you have the [OBSESSION/COMPULSION]?

What effect has it had on your life?

Has it affected your job (school)?....marriage?....relationship with friends?....social life?....leisure activities?
IF YES: In what way?

Does it keep you from completing your daily routine and chores?

How much time a day do you spend [OBSESSION/COMPULSION]?

(D)   <u>Exclude</u> the diagnosis if another axis I disorder is present, and the content of the obsessions or compulsions is restricted to it (e.g., preoccupation with food in the presence of an eating disorder; hair pulling in the presence of trichotillomania; concern with appearance in the presence of body dysmorphic disorder; preoccupation with having a serious illness in the presence of hypochondriasis).

(E)   <u>Exclude</u> the diagnosis if it is due to the direct physiological effect of a substance (e.g., a drug of abuse, a medication) or a general medical condition.

SOMATIZATION DISORDER

| Inclusion: A, B1-B4 |
| Exclusion: C |

(A) A history of many physical complaints beginning before age 30 years that occur over a period of several years and result in treatment being sought or significant impairment in social, occupational or other important areas of functioning.

How's your physical health been most of your life?
Do you get sick more than most people?
    IF EVIDENCE OF CHRONIC POOR HEALTH:
        What's been the matter?
        Would you say you've been sickly most of your life?
        Do you usually go to the doctor when you're feeling sick?
        About how many times a year do you go to the doctor? ER?
        What effect has your poor physical health had on your life?
        Has it effected your job (school)?....marriage?....relationship with friends?....social life? **IF YES:** In what way?

B. For a symptom to be counted towards the diagnosis, the symptom must not be fully explained by a known general medical condition or by the direct effect of a substance, or the resulting complaints or impairment from a general medical condition are in excess of what would be expected from the history, physical examination, or laboratory findings.

Follow-up questions for positive responses:
    Did you go to the doctor for that?
    What did the doctor say was wrong?
    What problems did the [SYMPTOM] cause you?

(B1) Four pain symptoms:

Have you had a lot of trouble with...
    (1) ...abdominal or belly pain (other than when menstruating)?
    (2) ...pain in your arms or legs? (7) chest pain?
    (3) ...back pain?   (8) pain during sex?
    (4) ...pain in your joints?   (9) excessively painful
    (5) ...pain when you urinate?   menstrual periods?
    (6) ...headaches?   (10) pain anywhere else?

(B2) Two gastrointestinal symptoms (other than pain):

Have you had a lot of trouble with...
      (1)   ...vomiting (other than during pregnancy)?
      (2)   ...nausea without vomiting (other than motion sickness)?
      (3)   ...excess gas or bloating of your stomach?
      (4)   ...diarrhea?
      (5)   ...foods you cannot eat because they make you ill?

(B3) One sexual symptom (other than pain):

      (1)   In general, has your sex life been important to you, or could
             you have gotten along as well without it?

FOR MEN ONLY:
      (2)   Has there ever been a time when you had trouble having an
             erection?
             Have you ever had difficulty ejaculating?
                IF YES: What caused the problem?

FOR WOMEN ONLY:
      (3)   Have your periods usually been pretty regular or irregular?
                IF IRREGULAR: Are they more irregular than most women?

      (4)   Do you usually bleed very heavy?
                IF YES: More than most women?

      (5)   **IF NOT ALREADY KNOWN:** Have you ever been pregnant?
                IF YES: What were your pregnancies like?
                           Did you ever have a lot of problems with vomiting?
                              IF YES: Did you vomit throughout any of your
                              pregnancies?

***DIAGNOSTIC REMINDER: For a symptom to be counted towards the diagnosis, the symptom must meet the general criteria for B described on page 61.

(B4) One pseudoneurologic symptom:

Did you ever...

    (1) ...have a period of amnesia--like a blackout or a lost period of time where you couldn't remember what happened?

    (2) ...have difficulty swallowing?

    (3) ...have shortness of breath when not exerting yourself?

    (4) ...lose your voice?

    (5) ...go complete deaf for a short while?

    (6) ...have double vision (not due to needing glasses)?

    (7) ...go totally blind for a short while?

    (8) ...faint?

    (9) ...have a seizure or convulsion?

    (10) ...have problems with numbness? **IF YES:** Where?

    (11) ...have trouble walking?

    (12) ...have problems with your balance or coordination?

    (13) ...have problems with muscle weakness so that you couldn't lift or move things like normal, or paralysis when you were completely unable to move a part of your body?

    (14) ...go a whole day without urinating?

(C) **Exclude** the diagnosis if the symptoms are intentionally produced or feigned (as in factitious disorder or malingering).

HYPOCHONDRIASIS

Inclusion: A, B, D, E
Exclusion: C, F

(A) **Preoccupation with fears of having, or the idea that one has, a serious disease based on the person's misinterpretation of bodily symptoms.**

How is your physical health?
(Do you have any physical problems?)

Do you worry a lot about your physical health?
  IF YES: What do you think might be wrong?
        How hard is it to get your mind off of this?

Do you often worry about the possibility that you have some type of serious illness?
  IF YES:
    What symptoms do you have that make you worry about this?
    What do you think might be wrong?
    How hard is it to get your mind off of this?

(B) **The preoccupation persists despite appropriate medical evaluation and reassurance.**

Did you see a doctor about these problems?
  IF YES: What kind of evaluation did he/she do?

What did your medical doctor say was the matter?

Did he/she have a diagnosis?

IF DOCTOR SAID THERE WAS NO EVIDENCE OF SERIOUS MEDICAL PROBLEM:
  How did that make you feel?
  Did you believe him/her?
  Is it hard for you to believe your doctor when he/she tells you there is nothing to worry about?
  Did you stop thinking about [PHYSICAL PROBLEM]?
    IF YES: After awhile, do you start thinking that you might be ill again?

(C) <u>Exclude</u> the diagnosis if the belief is of delusional intensity (as in delusional disorder, somatic type), and is not restricted to a circumscribed concern about appearance (as in body dysmorphic disorder).

   Is it possible that you don't have [DISEASE]?
      IF NO: Are you sure?
               Then why do you think the doctor hasn't diagnosed it?

(D) **The preoccupation causes clinically significant distress or impairment in social, occupational, or other important areas of functioning.**

   What effect has your worrying (or thinking) about having [PHYSICAL ILLNESS] had on your life?

   How upsetting has it been?

   Does it bother you a lot that you have these concerns?

   Has this affected your job (school)?....marriage?....relationship with friends?....social life?....leisure activities?
      IF YES: In what way?

   Does it interfere with or keep you from completing your daily routine and chores?

(E) **The duration of the disturbance is at least six months.**

   For how long have you been worrying or thinking about this?

(F) <u>Exclude</u> the diagnosis if the preoccupation is better accounted for by generalized anxiety disorder, obsessive-compulsive disorder, panic disorder, a major depressive episode, separation anxiety, or another somatoform disorder.

BODY DYSMORPHIC DISORDER

Inclusion: A, B
Exclusion: C

(A) **Preoccupation with an imagined defect in appearance. If a slight physical anomaly is present, the person's concern is markedly excessive.**

Do you often think there is something wrong with the way you look?

Do you often think you look gross, disfigured, or ugly?
    IF YES TO EITHER: To what are you referring?
                How much do you think about this?
                How hard is it to get your mind off of this?
                Have you talked to your friends or family about this?
                    IF YES: What do they say?
                        Do they try to convince you that you are wrong and that you don't look the way you think you do?

(B) **The preoccupation causes clinically significant distress or impairment in social, occupational, or other important areas of functioning.**

What difficulties in your life has your concern about your appearance caused?

Has it caused problems in your job (school)?....marriage?
....relationships with friends or family?....social life?....leisure activities?
    IF YES TO ANY: What kind of problems?
    IF NO TO ALL: Have you been socially withdrawn because of your concern about your appearance?

Have you seen a doctor to fix your [PHYSICAL DEFECT]?
    IF YES: What did the doctor recommend or do?

Did you ever have surgery?

(C) <u>Exclude</u> the diagnosis if the preoccupation is better accounted for by another mental disorder (e.g., dissatisfaction with body shape and size in anorexia nervosa).

INTERMITTENT EXPLOSIVE DISORDER

Inclusion: A, B
Exclusion: C

(A) **Several discrete episodes of failure to resist aggressive impulses that result in serious assaultive acts or destruction of property.**

Now I'd like to ask you some questions about your temper and violent behavior. Do you have an explosive or violent temper?

Have you ever "lost control" and either seriously assaulted someone or destroyed property?
   IF YES: How many times has this happened?
            What types of things did you do?

(B) **The degree of aggressiveness expressed during the episodes is grossly out of proportion to any precipitating psychosocial stressors.**

What usually leads up to these explosions? (Give examples)

Do you think your reaction was unreasonable or excessive?

(C) **<u>Exclude</u> the diagnosis if the episodes of aggressiveness are better accounted for by another mental disorder (e.g., antisocial or borderline personality disorder, a psychotic disorder, a manic episode, conduct disorder, or attention deficit hyperactivity disorder), or are due to the direct physiological effects of a substance (e.g., a drug of abuse, a medication), or a general medical condition (e.g., personality change due to head trauma, Alzheimer's disease).**

TRICHOTILLOMANIA

Inclusion: A, B, C, E
Exclusion: D

(A) Recurrent pulling out of one's hair resulting in noticeable hair loss.

Do you frequently pull out your hair from your head, eyebrows, or other parts of your body?
>**IF YES:** From what parts of your body do you pull your hair?
>Do you pull out enough so that it is noticeable (to others)?

(B) An increasing sense of tension immediately before pulling out the hair or when attempting to resist the behavior.

Do you feel compelled to pull out your hair?
>**IF YES:** Describe what that's like.

Do you get somewhat tense or anxious immediately before you pull?

Do you get tense or anxious when you try to resist pulling?

(C) Pleasure, gratification, or relief when pulling out the hair.

How do you feel immediately after you pull?

Is there any sense of pleasure?

What about tension release or relief?

(D) Exclude the diagnosis if it is better accounted for by another mental disorder or it is due to a general medical condition (e.g., a dermatological disorder.)

(E) The disturbance causes clinically significant distress or impairment in social, occupational, or other important areas of functioning.

What effect has the hair pulling had on your life?

How upsetting is it? Does it bother you a lot that you do this?

Has this affected your job (school)?....marriage?....relationship with friends?...social life?...leisure activities? **IF YES:** In what way?

Does it interfere with or keep you from completing your daily routine and chores?

Childhood Disorders

ATTENTION-DEFICIT/HYPERACTIVITY DISORDER

> Inclusion: A1 or A2, B, C, D
> Exclusion: E

A. EITHER (A1) OR (A2):

A1. Inattention: At least six of the following symptoms of inattention have persisted for at least six months to a degree that is maladaptive and inconsistent with developmental level:

```
************************************************************
    NOTE: For each symptom you must inquire whether it is present
          more than most boys/girls the child's age.
************************************************************
```

(1) Often fails to give close attention to details or makes careless mistakes in schoolwork, work, or other activities.

Some kids have problems paying close attention to things, and because of this they make a lot of careless mistakes in their schoolwork. Is this something you do?
    IF YES: Does it happen a lot?
              Does it affect your grades?
What about things around the house. Do you often make careless mistakes when doing chores around the house?
    IF YES: Examples.

(2) Often has difficulty sustaining attention in tasks or play activities.

Some kids have a hard time staying on track or keeping their mind on the things they are doing because they can't pay attention to one thing for a long time. Is it hard for you to pay attention to only one thing for a long time?

Is it hard for you to stick with one thing, even when it's fun?

Is it hard to focus on a test or an assignment that lasts an entire period?

Is it hard to play a game that lasts a long time like Monopoly?
    IF YES TO ANY: Do you frequently have difficulty focusing on one thing for a long time?
                    Does your poor attention span cause you difficulties?

---

(3) **Often does not seem to listen when spoken to directly.**

How good are you at listening to what your parents or teachers say to you?

Do your teachers say that you don't listen when they talk to you?

Do they have to ask you the same thing over and over before you listen?

What about with your parents. Do they often have to repeat what they say to you? Do they sometimes say you "must be deaf?"
    IF EVIDENCE OF POOR LISTENING:
        How often does this happen?

---

(4) **Often does not follow through on instructions and fails to finish schoolwork, chores, or duties in the workplace (not due to oppositional behavior or failure to understand instructions).**

Some kids have difficulty finishing things. Is that true of you?

Is it hard to finish your homework or schoolwork, even when you know how to do it?
    IF YES: Is it hard to stick with it, or do you stop doing it because you don't like doing it?

What about things around the house. Do you start doing them and leave in the middle?
    IF YES: Do you do that a lot?
        Is it hard to stick with it, or do you stop doing it because you don't like doing it?

---

(5) **Often has difficulty organizing tasks and activities.**

Is it hard for you to be organized?
    IF YES: Tell me about that.

Is it difficult for you to plan and organize your schoolwork?
    IF YES: What happens?

Do you need your mom's or dad's help getting organized to do school projects?
    IF YES: What would happen?

---

(6)   Often avoids, dislikes, or is reluctant to engage in tasks that require sustained mental effort (such as schoolwork or homework).

Some kids really hate doing schoolwork or homework because it's hard for them to concentrate on it for a long time. Are you like that?

---

(7)   Often loses things necessary for tasks or activities (e.g., school assignments, pencils, books, tools, or toys).

Do you lose things a lot?

At school do you frequently forget your pen or pencil, or leave your books or homework in the wrong place?

What about toys, keys, and money? Do you lose or misplace them a lot?

---

(8)   Is often easily distracted by extraneous stimuli.

Some kids find it hard to keep their mind on the things they are doing, even when it's fun. Is it hard for you to keep playing a game when you hear something in the next room?
How easy is it for someone to get your attention when you're watching your favorite TV program?
> **IF DISTRACTED:** So, is it hard for you to focus on one activity
>   for a long time?
>   Does this happen a lot?
>   Does it happen at school? At home, too?

---

(9)   Is often forgetful in daily activities.

Are you very forgetful?
What types of things do you forget to do?
Do you often forget to do things like brushing your teeth, washing your hands, changing your underwear?
> **IF YES:** Is this forgetfulness, or is it that you don't like doing
>   these things?

A2. <u>Hyperactivity-Impulsivity</u>: At least six of the following symptoms of hyperactivity-impulsivity have persisted for at least six months to a degree that is maladaptive and inconsistent with developmental level:

---

(1) **Often fidgets with hands or feet or squirms in seat.**

Is it hard for you to sit still?

Is it hard to sit still while watching television, playing a game, or doing homework, or while you're sitting in class at school?

Has anyone ever said that you can't seem to sit still, or that it seems like you have "ants in your pants?"

---

(2) **Often leaves seat in classroom or in other situations in which remaining seated is expected.**

Is it hard for you to stay in your seat in school?

Do you get out of your seat a lot when you're not supposed to?
    IF YES: Tell me about that.
           Have you gotten into trouble for it?

Do you stay in your chair during all of breakfast or all of dinner, at home or at a restaurant, or do you get up a lot?

---

(3) **Often runs about or climbs excessively in situations in which it is inappropriate (in adolescents or adults, may be limited to subjective feelings of restlessness).**

Do you run around the house or climb on furniture a lot?

Do you climb on desks or other things in school?

Do you jump down the stairs or run down the halls?
    IF YES TO ANY: Tell me about it.
                Do your teachers/parents often have to tell you to stop running around so much?
                Do you get into trouble for this? Does it happen a lot?

---

(4)   Often has difficulty playing or engaging in leisure activities quietly.

Do your parents frequently tell you to quiet down when you play?
Are you noisier than other kids your age?
Is this a problem at school?

---

(5)   Is often "on the go" or acts as if "driven by a motor".

Are you often on the go, doing something?
Are you more active than other kids your age?
Does it feel like there's a motor inside you that keeps you going all the time?

---

(6)   Often talks excessively.

Do you talk a lot? **IF YES:** More than other kids?

Do your parents or teachers say that you're a chatterbox because you never stop talking?

---

(7)   Often blurts out answers before questions have been completed.

When your teachers ask questions in class do you tend to answer the question out loud before the teacher has a chance to finish asking it?
    IF YES: How often does this happen?
                Has your teacher spoken to you or your parents about this?

---

(8)   Often has difficulty awaiting turn.

For some kids it is hard for them to wait their turn when playing games. Is this hard for you?
    IF YES: What problems does this cause?

Is it hard for you to wait on line in stores, or going to movies, or other activities where you have to wait on line?
Do you often try to cut in line?

When you eat with your family is it hard for you to wait to get served?
    IF YES: Do other people get angry with you because of this?

(9) **Often interrupts or intrudes on others (e.g., butts into conversations or games).**

Do your parents get angry at you because you butt into their conversations?

Do your parents get angry because you interrupt them while they're on the phone?
IF YES: Does this happen a lot?

Do other kids tell you to leave them alone so they could do their work?

Do you butt into other kids games before they ask you to play?

(B) **Some hyperactive-impulsive or inattentive symptoms that caused impairment were present before age seven years.**

IF TIME COURSE NOT ALREADY ESTABLISHED:
How old were you when you began (BEHAVIORS NOTED ABOVE)? What problems did this cause?

(C) **Some impairment from the symptoms is present in two or more settings (e.g., at school [or work] and at home).**

(D) **There must be clear evidence of clinically significant impairment in social, academic, or occupational functioning.**

IF IMPAIRMENT NOT ALREADY ESTABLISHED:
What problems do (BEHAVIORS NOTED ABOVE) cause?
Do (BEHAVIORS) bother your parents a lot?
Does it cause school problems?
What problems does it cause with other kids?
Did you see a doctor or school counselor or anyone else like that?
Did you take medication for (BEHAVIORS)?

(E) <u>Exclude</u> **the diagnosis if it occurs exclusively during the course of a pervasive developmental disorder, schizophrenia or other psychotic disorder, and is not better accounted for by another mental disorder (e.g., a mood disorder, anxiety disorder, dissociative disorder, or a personality disorder).**

CONDUCT DISORDER

> Inclusion: At least 3 from A, B
> Exclusion: C

Now I'm going to ask you about some different types of behaviors that sometimes get children and teenagers into trouble.

A. A repetitive and persistent pattern of behavior in which the basic rights of others or major age-appropriate societal norms or rules are violated, as manifested by the presence of at least three of the following criteria in the past twelve months, with at least one criterion present in the past six months.

AGGRESSION TO PEOPLE AND ANIMALS

(A1) Often bullies, threatens, or intimidates others.

Do you pick on other kids?
    IF YES: How often?
            Do you pick on kids that are younger or smaller than you? Describe.

Are you a bully?

Do you ever threaten other kids so they will buy you things, give you money, or do other things for you?
    IF YES: How often? Describe.

(A2) Often initiates physical fights.

Do you get into many fights? (More than other kids?)
    IF YES: How often?
            How often do you start the fights?

(A3) Has used a weapon that can cause serious physical harm to others (e.g., a bat, brick, broken bottle, knife, gun).

Have you ever used a weapon in a fight?
    IF YES: What did you use?
            For what reason?
            How often did that happen?

(A4) Has been physically cruel to people.

Have you hurt people physically?
IF YES: What did you do to them? For what reason?

(A5) Has been physically cruel to animals.

Have you ever hurt, tortured, or killed an animal?
IF YES: What did you do?

Do you have a pet?
IF YES: Did you ever deliberately hurt it?

(A6) Has stolen while confronting a victim (e.g., mugging, purse snatching, extortion, armed robbery).

Have you ever taken things from people like snatching a purse, jewelry, or chains?

Have you ever held anyone up, or robbed a store?

Have you ever threatened anyone if they didn't give you money?

(A7) Has forced someone into sexual activity.

Have you ever forced anyone to have sex with you?

Were you ever part of a group or gang that forced someone to have sex against his/her will?
IF YES: Tell me about that.

DESTRUCTION OF PROPERTY

(A8) Has deliberately engaged in fire setting with the intention of causing serious damage.

Have you ever set things on fire?
IF YES: Why?

(A9) Has deliberately destroyed others' property (other than by fire setting).

Have you ever damaged someone's property by breaking windows, spraying graffiti on walls, or other things like that?
IF YES: What did you do?

DECEITFULNESS OR THEFT

(A10) Has broken into someone else's house, building, or car.

> Have you ever broken into anyone's house, a store, building or car?
> **IF YES:** For what reason?
> > Did you do it alone or with someone?

(A11) Often lies to obtain goods or favors or to avoid obligations (i.e., "cons" others).

> Sometimes kids don't tell the truth; they make up stories. Do you make up stories that aren't truthful?
> **IF YES:** What kinds of things do you make up stories about?
>
> Do you tell a lot of lies?
> **IF YES:** Do you lie a lot or a little?
>
> Do you often lie to get things that you wanted?
>
> Do you often lie to avoid chores or other responsibilities?

(A12) Has stolen items of nontrivial value without confronting a victim (e.g., shoplifting, burglary, forgery).

> How often have you stolen from stores, your parents, or other people?
> **IF YES:** What did you steal?
> > What's the most you've stolen?
>
> Did you ever get caught stealing?
> **IF YES:** What happened?
>
> Did you ever pick anyone's pocket, write a forged check, or use a credit card without permission?

SERIOUS VIOLATIONS OF RULES

(A13) Often stays out all night despite parental prohibitions, beginning before 13 years of age.

Do you argue with your parents about how late you could stay out at night?

Do you often stay out later than they said you could?

Did you ever stay out all night?
   IF YES: How old were you when you first began doing this?

(A14) Has run away from home overnight at least twice while living in parental or parental surrogate home (or once without returning for a lengthy period).

Did you ever run away from home overnight?
   IF YES: How often?
            How long did you stay away?

(A15) Is often truant from school, beginning before 13 years of age.

Have you ever played hooky or skipped school?
   IF YES: How many times did you do it?
            Did you get into trouble for it?
            How old were you?
            How old were you when you started to skip school?

(B)   The disturbance in behavior causes significant impairment in social, academic, or occupational functioning.

You mentioned that you (BEHAVIORS ACKNOWLEDGED ABOVE).

What problems did this cause?

Does it cause problems at school? (Expulsion? Suspension?)

How does it affect your friendships, or family life?

Have you ever seen a doctor, counselor, or anyone else for this?

(C)   <u>Exclude</u> the diagnosis if age 18 or older and meets criteria for antisocial personality disorder.

OPPOSITIONAL DEFIANT DISORDER

Inclusion: At least 4 from A, B
Exclusion: C, D

****
NOTE: For each symptom you must inquire whether it is present
more than most boys/girls the child's age.
****

A. **A pattern of negativistic, hostile, and defiant behavior lasting at least six months, during which time at least four of the following are present:**

(A1) Often loses temper.

What happens when you get angry and mad?

Does this happen a lot?

Do you have a bad temper?
   IF YES: Tell me about that.

Is your temper so big that you can't stop it?

Do you have temper tantrums?
   IF YES: What causes them?
         How often do you have them?

(A2) Often argues with adults.

Do you frequently argue with your parents or teachers?
   IF YES: About what?
         Do you always find something to argue about?

(A3) Often actively defies or refuses to comply with adults' requests or rules.

Is it hard for you to follow rules?

Do you think that most rules are pretty stupid?
   IF YES: Tell me about that.

Do you like to break rules on purpose?

Do you often say no when your parents or teachers ask you to do something?
   IF YES: Like what?

(A4) Often deliberately annoys people.

Do you like to do things that annoy or bother other people?
  IF YES: Like what?
       How often do you do things like that?

(A5) Often blames others for his or her mistakes or misbehavior.

Is it hard for you to admit that you are wrong when you make a mistake?

Do you blame other people for your mistakes?

Do you blame other people when you misbehave or get into trouble?

(A6) Is often touchy or easily annoyed by others.

What do your parents or teachers do that bothers you?

Is it easy for others to annoy you?

(A7) Is often angry and resentful.

Do you feel angry a lot of the time?
  IF YES: Why is that?

Does it often bother you that other people boss you around or tell you what to do?
  IF YES: Tell me about that.

Do you think that you are treated unfairly?
  IF YES: By whom?
       In what way?

(A8) Is often spiteful or vindictive.

IF YES TO ANY QUESTION IN #7:
  What do you do about _____?
  How do you get back at _____?

(B)   The disturbance in behavior causes significant impairment in social, academic, or occupational functioning.

You mentioned that you (BEHAVIORS ACKNOWLEDGED ABOVE).

What problems did this cause?

Does it cause problems at school? (Suspension? Transfer?)

Has it caused you to lose friends?

What about problems at home?

Have you ever seen a doctor, counselor, or anyone else for this?

(C)   Exclude the diagnosis if behaviors occur exclusively during the course of a psychotic or mood disorder.

(D)   Exclude the diagnosis if person meets criteria for conduct disorder or, if age 18 or older, meets criteria for antisocial personality disorder.

SEPARATION ANXIETY DISORDER

Inclusion: At least 3 from A, B, C, D
Exclusion: E

A. **Developmentally inappropriate and excessive anxiety concerning separation from home or from those to whom the child is attached, as evidenced by at least three of the following:**

(A1) Persistent and excessive worry about losing, or possible harm befalling, major attachment figures.

(MAF = Major Attachment Figure, i.e., mother, father, etc.)

Do you worry a lot that something bad will happen to your MAF?

Do you worry a lot that they will go away and never come back?

Do you often get scared that they will get hurt or die?
   IF YES TO ANY: Why are you scared about that?
                     For how long have you been worrying about this?

(A2) Persistent and excessive worry that an untoward event will lead to separation from a major attachment figure (e.g., getting lost or being kidnapped).

Do you get scared a lot about getting lost when you leave the house with your MAF?

Do you get scared that your MAF will leave you and not come back?

Do you get scared that you or your MAF will be kidnapped and you'd never see them again?
   IF YES TO ANY: How often do you worry that _____?
                     For how long have you been worrying about this?

(A3) Persistent reluctance or refusal to go to school or elsewhere because of fear of separation.

Do you get any nervous or scared feelings about going to school?
IF YES: Tell me about that.

When you first started going to school was it hard for you to go because you didn't want to be away from your MAF?
IF YES: Did they have to drag you to school?
Did you refuse to go?

(A4) Persistently and excessively fearful or reluctant to be alone or without major attachment figures at home or without significant adults in other settings.

Is it scary for you to be alone at home?

Do you feel upset if an adult isn't always with you?
IF YES TO EITHER: How old were you when you started to feel this way?

(A5) Persistent reluctance or refusal to go to sleep without being near a major attachment figure or sleep away from home.

Do you sleep alone or with your parents?
Are you afraid of going to sleep alone?
Does your MAF have to stay nearby or with you till you fall asleep?
Is it hard to sleep when your MAF isn't around?
Do you sometimes not go to sleep until your MAF is in the home?

Are you allowed to sleep at someone else's house?
IF YES: Have you ever been invited to stay at someone's house?
IF YES: Did you go?
IF NO: Why not?
IF YES: How was it being away from your MAF?

(A6) Repeated nightmares involving the theme of separation.

Do you have a lot of scary dreams or nightmares?
IF YES: What are they about?
(Do you have any about being separated from you MAF - like being kidnapped or your MAF going away?)

(A7) **Repeated complaints of physical symptoms (such as headaches, stomachaches, nausea, or vomiting) when separation from major attachment figure occurs or is anticipated.**

Do you get physically sick when you are not with your MAF?

Do you often get sick before you go to school in the morning?

Do you get physically sick thinking that your MAF is going somewhere without you?

IF YES TO ANY: What part of your body gets sick?

How often does this happen?

(A8) **Recurrent excessive distress when separation from home or major attachment figure occurs or is anticipated.**

Do you get upset or nervous when you are away from home?

Do you get upset when you see your MAF going out without you?

Do you get upset just thinking that your MAF is going somewhere without you?

IF YES TO ANY: What do you do? (Call home? Go home early? Cry? Scream? Have a temper tantrum?)

(B) **Duration of the disturbance is at least four weeks.**

IF NOT CLEAR FROM ABOVE INFORMATION:

For how long have you (SYMPTOMS NOTED ABOVE)?

(C) **Onset before age 18.**

(D) **The disturbance causes clinically significant distress or impairment in social, academic (occupational), or other important areas of functioning.**

What problems have the (BEHAVIORS NOTED ABOVE) caused?

Have your grades suffered or have you missed a lot of school?

Has it affected the number of friends you have?

Have you ever see a doctor, counselor, or anyone else for this?

(E) **Exclude the diagnosis if the symptoms occur exclusively during the course of a pervasive developmental disorder, schizophrenia, or other psychotic disorder, and in adults and adolescents, is not better accounted for by panic disorder with agoraphobia.**

Axis II Personality Disorders

PARANOID PD

Inclusion: At least 4 from A
Exclusion: B

A. **A pervasive distrust and suspiciousness of others such that their motives are interpreted as malevolent, beginning by early adulthood and present in a variety of contexts, as indicated by at least four of the following:**

(A1) Suspects, without sufficient basis, that others are exploiting, harming, or deceiving him or her.

Have you had experiences where people who pretended to be your friends took advantage of you?
IF YES: What happened? How often has this happened?

Are you good at spotting someone who is trying to deceive or con you?
IF YES: How can you tell?

Are you concerned that someone might be trying to hurt you?
IF YES: Tell me about that.

(A2) Is preoccupied with unjustified doubts about the loyalty or trustworthiness of friends or associates.

Are you concerned that certain friends or coworkers are not really loyal or trustworthy?
IF YES: How much time do you think about this?
What has caused your concern?
Has this made your life difficult?

(A3) Is reluctant to confide in others because of unwarranted fear that the information will be used maliciously against him or her.

Some people are very reluctant to confide in other people. Are you like this?
IF YES: Why is that?

Do you usually find there's often a price to pay when you've shared something personal with others?
IF YES: Does this keep you from opening up to others?
What might happen if you did confide?

(A4) Reads hidden demeaning or threatening meanings into benign remarks or events.

Do people frequently seem to do things just to annoy you?
  IF YES: Like what?

Do you usually take what people tell you at face value, or do you frequently try to figure out what they really mean?
  IF FIGURE OUT: What kinds of things do you think they really mean?
  Do their comments often turn out to be hidden threats or put downs?

(A5) Persistently bears grudges, i.e., unforgiving of insults, injuries, or slights.

How long would you stay angry at someone who does something to hurt or insult you like not inviting you to a party?

Do you tend to hold grudges?
If someone insults you, how long does it take until you forgive them?
Are there any people you've never forgiven?
  IF YES: Can you tell me about it?

(A6) Perceives attacks on his or her character or reputation that are not apparent to others and is quick to react angrily or counterattack.

Do people say things to attack your character or ruin your reputation, even though it might not seem that way to others?
  IF YES: Tell me about that.
  How do you react to this?

Do you find that people often make indirect comments to attack you or put you down, rather than tell you directly?
  IF YES: How do you react?
  Do you get angry?
  Do you try to get back at the person?

Do other people say that you read too much into things and take offense at things that were not meant to be critical?
  IF YES: Example?

(A7) Has recurrent suspicions, without justification, regarding fidelity of spouse or sexual partner.

When you've been involved in a relationship, do you often worry that your partner is unfaithful to you?
   IF YES: What causes your concern?
             How did it turn out?

(B) <u>Exclude</u> the diagnosis if the features only occurred during the course of schizophrenia, a mood disorder with psychotic features, or another psychotic disorder, and are not due to the direct physiological effects of a general medical condition.

SCHIZOID PD

> Inclusion: At least 4 from A
> Exclusion: B

A. **A pervasive pattern of detachment from social relationships and a restricted range of expression of emotions in interpersonal settings, beginning by early adulthood and present in a variety of contexts, as indicated by at least four of the following:**

(A1) **Neither desires nor enjoys close relationships, including being part of a family.**

> Do you have any close relationships with friends or family?
> **IF YES:** With whom?
> What do you enjoy about these relationships?
> **IF NO:** Does this bother you?
> Do you wish you had some close relationships?

(A2) **Almost always chooses solitary activities.**

> Some people prefer to spend time with other people, while others prefer to work and do things alone. How would you describe yourself?
> **IF ALONE:** Do you almost always choose to do things by yourself?

(A3) **Has little, if any, interest in having sexual experiences with another person.**

> In general, has your sex life been important to you, or could you have gotten along as well without it?
> **IF SAYS NOT IMPORTANT OR NOT CURRENTLY INVOLVED:**
> Would it bother you to live your entire life without sexual relationships?

(A4) **Takes pleasure in few, if any, activities.**

> What kinds of activities do you enjoy?
> **IF ONLY 1 OR 2 ARE MENTIONED:**
> If [ACTIVITIES MENTIONED] were not available, are there any other things you would enjoy doing?

(A5) Lacks close friends or confidants other than first-degree relatives.

Not counting your immediate family, do you have any close friends you can confide in?

(A6) Appears indifferent to the praise or criticism of others.

How do you react when someone criticizes you?
   IF NO REACTION: So you don't look or feel upset after you are
        criticized?

How do you react when someone compliments you?
   IF NO REACTION: So you don't smile or think about it later and
        feel good about it?

(A7) Shows emotional coldness, detachment, or flattened affectivity.

[NOTE OBSERVATIONS]
[Is (s)he slow to look you in the eye when talking?]
[Does (s)he usually smile or nod back at you during
conversation?]
[Can you tell what (s)he is feeling by the expression on his/her
face?]

(B)   <u>Exclude</u> the diagnosis if the features only occurred during the course of schizophrenia, a mood disorder with psychotic features, or another psychotic disorder, and are not due to the direct physiological effects of a general medical condition.

SCHIZOTYPAL PD

Inclusion: At least 5 from A
Exclusion: B

A. A pervasive pattern of social and interpersonal deficits marked by acute discomfort with, and reduced capacity for, close relationships as well as by cognitive or perceptual distortions and eccentricities of behavior, beginning by early adulthood and present in a variety of contexts, as indicated by at least five of the following:

(A1) Ideas of reference (excluding delusions of reference).

Have you ever found that people around you seem to be talking in general, but then you realize their comments are really meant for you?
  IF YES: How do you know they are talking about you?

When you walk into a room, does it sometimes seem like people stop talking or act differently?
  IF YES: How often does this happen?

Have you ever noticed that someone in charge changed the rules specifically because of you, but they wouldn't admit it?

Do you sometimes feel like strangers on the street are looking at you or talking about you?
  IF YES: Why do you think they notice you in particular?

(A2) Odd beliefs or magical thinking, that influence behavior and are inconsistent with subcultural norms, (e.g., superstitiousness, belief in clairvoyance, telepathy, or "sixth sense;" in children and adolescents, bizarre fantasies or preoccupations).

A number of people talk about having telepathy or ESP and feel like they can sense what's in someone's mind or predict the future. Have you had any experiences like this?
  IF YES: How often? Are these experiences very important to your life?
        IF YES: How? Have your friends and family also had experiences like this?

Are you a superstitious person?

    IF YES: In what way?

            How does this influence decisions you make or your behavior?

            Do your friends and family share these superstitions?

Some people believe they can influence things like the weather or ball games just by thinking about them. Do you believe that you can make things happen just by thinking about them?

    IF YES: Tell me about it.

Do you believe in hexes, curses, omens, voodoo, witchcraft, magic, or other things like this?

    IF YES: Tell me about that.

            Have any of these things influenced your decisions or behavior?

            Do your friends and family share these beliefs?

(A3) Unusual perceptual experiences, including bodily illusions.

Have you ever sensed there was some unusual force or presence in the room?

    IF YES: Can you describe what this was like?

            What do you think caused this?

            How often has this happened?

Have you ever felt like the world around you looked or seemed different than it usually does?

Have colors or shapes ever seemed changed or different than normal?

    IF YES TO EITHER: What was this like?

                       Were you using any drugs or alcohol at the time?

Do your eyes ever play tricks on you--for instance, someone's face or body suddenly seems to change in shape or form?

    IF YES: Can you tell me about this?

Do you ever mistake noises for voices, or shadows or objects for people?

    IF YES: How often does this happen?

(A4) Odd thinking and speech (e.g., vague, circumstantial, metaphorical, overelaborate, or stereotyped).

[NOTE OBSERVATIONS]
  [Does (s)he seem to talk in an odd or unusual way?]
    IF YES: How so?
  [When (s)he talks about something, do you find it hard to follow what (s)he is saying?]

(A5) Suspiciousness or paranoid ideation.

Have you had experiences where people who pretended to be your friends took advantage of you?
  IF YES: What happened?
          How often has this happened?

Do you often worry that people might be planning to harm or take advantage of you?
  IF YES: Why do you think that?

Are you reluctant to confide in others because the information might be used against you?
  IF YES: What caused this concern?

Do you usually take what people tell you at face value, or do you frequently try to figure out what they really mean?
  IF YES: What kinds of things do you think they really mean?
          Do the comments often turn out to be hidden threats or put downs?

Do other people say that you read too much into things and take offense at things that were not meant to be critical?
  IF YES: Example?

(A6) Inappropriate or constricted affect.

[NOTE OBSERVATIONS]
  [Is there anything peculiar about the way (s)he shows his/her emotions?]
  [Does it seem like (s)he never expresses any emotion?]
  [Does (s)he often laugh or smile for no good reason?]
  [Does it often seem like the emotion (s)he is showing does not fit with what (s)he is saying?]

(A7) Behavior or appearance that is odd, eccentric, or peculiar.

[NOTE OBSERVATIONS]
[Is there anything odd or peculiar about the way (s)he looks?]
[Does (s)he dress in an odd or peculiar way that is not explained by current fashion trends?]
> IF YES: Do you think (s)he dresses this way to attract attention? (RATING NOTE: SCHIZOTYPES GENERALLY DO NOT DRESS TO GET ATTENTION)

[Does (s)he do odd or peculiar things?]
[Does (s)he often talk to him/herself?]

(A8) Lacks close friends or confidants other than first-degree relatives.

Not counting your immediate family, do you have any close friends you can confide in?

(A9) Excessive social anxiety that does not diminish with familiarity and tends to be associated with paranoid fears rather than negative judgements about self.

Do you generally feel nervous or anxious around people?
> IF YES: How bad does it get?
> What makes you nervous?
> Do you get nervous around people because you are worried about what they might do to you, or is it because you don't feel you're as good as other people?
> Do you avoid situations where you have to meet new people?
> Are you less nervous after you get to know people better?

(B) <u>Exclude</u> the diagnosis if the features only occurred during the course of schizophrenia, a mood disorder with psychotic features, or another psychotic disorder.

BORDERLINE PD

Inclusion: At least 5 criteria
Exclusion: None

A pervasive pattern of instability of interpersonal relationships, self-image, and affects, and marked impulsivity beginning by early adulthood and present in a variety of contexts, as indicated by at least five of the following:

---

(1) Frantic efforts to avoid real or imagined abandonment. [Do not include suicidal or self-mutilating behavior covered in criterion 5].

Have there been times when you've been very upset, almost to the point of being distraught, because you thought someone you loved or needed very much might leave you?
    IF YES: How often has this happened?
        What did you do to keep them from leaving?
           IF ONLY SUICIDAL/SELF-MUTILATING BEHAVIOR:
              What else have you done?

Do you spend a lot of time thinking of ways to keep people from leaving you?

---

(2) A pattern of unstable and intense interpersonal relationships characterized by alternating between extremes of idealization and devaluation.

Do your relationships with friends and lovers tend to be intense and stormy with lots of ups and downs?
    IF YES: Can you tell me about some of them?

With some people do you switch from loving, respecting, and admiring them at one time, to despising them at another time?
    IF YES: Tell me about that.

---

(3) Identity disturbance: markedly and persistently unstable self-image or sense of self.

Does the way you think about yourself change so often that you don't know who you are? **IF YES:** Tell me about this.

Do you ever feel like you're someone else, or that you're evil, or maybe that you don't even exist? **IF PRESENT:** Tell me about that.

---

(4)   **Impulsivity in at least two areas that are potentially self-damaging (e.g., spending, sex, substance abuse, reckless driving, binge eating) NOTE: DO NOT INCLUDE SUICIDAL OR SELF-MUTILATING BEHAVIOR COVERED IN CRITERION 5.**

I am going to read you a list of behaviors that sometimes cause problems for people. How many times in the past 5 years have you...

   a) gambled more money than you could afford to lose?
   b) spent money impulsively on things you didn't need or couldn't afford?
   c) had one night stands or brief sexual affairs?
   d) been intoxicated with alcohol?
   e) been stoned or high on other drugs?
   f) shoplifted or took something that didn't belong to you?
   g) been in an auto accident, received a speeding ticket, or been charged with reckless driving?
   h) driven while intoxicated or high?
   i) gone on eating binges (ate a large amount of food in a short time and felt like you lost control of your eating)?
   j) done anything else impulsive where you could have gotten hurt?

---

(5)   **Recurrent suicidal behavior, gestures, or threats, or self-mutilating behavior.**

Have you ever been so upset that you told someone that you wanted to hurt or kill yourself?
   IF YES: Tell me about it.
            How often have you done this?

Have you ever made a suicide attempt, even one that wasn't very serious?
   IF YES: What did you do?
            How many attempts have you made?

Have you ever been so upset or tense that you deliberately hurt yourself by cutting your skin, putting your hand through a glass window, burning yourself, or anything else like this?
   IF YES: What have you done?
            How often?

---

(6)   Affective instability due to a marked reactivity of mood (e.g., intense episodic dysphoria, irritability, or anxiety usually lasting a few hours and only rarely more than a few days).

Has anyone ever told you that you're irritable or that your moods seem to change a great deal?
IF YES: Tell me about it.

Do you often have days when your mood is constantly changing--days when you shift back and forth from feeling your usual self, to feeling angry or depressed or anxious?
IF PRESENT: Are the mood swings mild or very intense?
How often does this happen in a typical week?
How long do the moods last?

---

(7)   Chronic feelings of emptiness.

Do you feel empty much of the time?
IF YES: What percent of the time do you feel that way?

---

(8)   Inappropriate, intense anger or difficulty controlling anger (e.g., frequent displays of temper, constant anger, recurrent physical fights).

How easily do you lose your temper?
How often do you lose your temper?

Do you feel angry much of the time?
What kinds of things get you really angry?
Are you sometimes angry without knowing why you feel that way?

Tell me what you are like when you are very angry.
How long do you usually stay angry?

Do you ever throw or break things? Have you ever hit anyone? Do you get into physical fights?
IF YES TO ANY: Tell me about it.

When you are angry, do you ever give someone the silent treatment?
IF YES: How long can you keep it up?
Is that a common reaction for you?

(9) **Transient, stress-related paranoid ideation or severe dissociative symptoms.**

When some people are under stress, they may have experiences that are very hard to explain to other people. Have you ever felt like things around you were somehow strange, or changed in size or shape?
   IF YES: Describe what that is like.

When you've been under stress, have you ever felt like your body or a part of it was somehow changed or not real?

Have you ever felt like you were watching yourself from outside your body?
   IF YES: Describe what that was like.

Do you ever have brief blackouts and forget what has happened?

When you're feeling stressed, do you ever get paranoid or suspicious of people you usually trust?
   IF NO: What about being afraid that someone is spying on you or planning to hurt you?
         IF YES TO EITHER: Does this happen even when you're not stressed?

IF ANY OF ABOVE ARE POSITIVE, ASK:
   You've said that you (LIST DISSOCIATIVE OR PARANOID EXPERIENCES): Were you using drugs or alcohol when this happened?
      IF YES: Does this happen only when you're using drugs or alcohol?

IF OCCURS WHEN NOT USING DRUGS OR ALCOHOL:
   How long do these experiences last?
   Do they go away when you're not under stress?

ANTISOCIAL PD

> Inclusion: A, At least 3 from B, at least 3 from C
> Exclusion: D

A. **Current age at least 18 years.**

B. **Evidence of Conduct Disorder with onset before age 15 as demonstrated by at least three of the following:**

(B1) **Often bullies, threatens or intimidates others.**

As a child or teenager did you pick on other kids?
  IF YES: How often?

Did you pick on kids that were younger or smaller than you?
  IF YES: Describe.

(B2) **Often initiates physical fights.**

Did you get into many fights? (More than other kids?)
  IF YES: How often? How often did you start the fights?

(B3) **Has used a weapon that can cause serious physical harm to others (e.g., a bat, brick, broken bottle, knife, gun).**

Did you ever use a weapon in a fight?
  IF YES: What did you use? For what reason?
      How often did that happen?

(B4) **Has stolen with confrontation with a victim (e.g., mugging, purse snatching, extortion, armed robbery).**

As a child or teenager, did you ever take things from people like snatching a purse, jewelry, or chains?

Did you ever hold anyone up, or rob a store?

Did you ever threaten anyone if they didn't give you money?

(B5) Has been physically cruel to people.

Did you hurt people when you weren't in a fight?
  IF YES: What did you do to them?
    For what reason?

(B6) Has been physically cruel to animals.

Did you ever hurt or kill an animal?
  IF YES: What did you do?

(B7) Has forced someone into sexual activity.

Did you ever force anyone to have sex with you?

Were you ever part of a group or gang that forced someone to have sex against his/her will?
  IF YES: Tell me about that.

(B8) Often lies or breaks promises to obtain goods or favors or to avoid obligations (e.g., "cons" others).

Did you tell a lot of lies?
  IF YES: For what reason(s)?
    Did you often lie to get things that you wanted?
    Did you often lie to avoid chores or other responsibilities?

(B9) Often stays out at night despite parental prohibitions, beginning before 13 years of age.

Did you argue with your parents about how late you could stay out at night?

Did you often stay out later than they said you could?

Did you ever stay out all night?
  IF YES: How old were you when you first began doing this?

(B10) **Has stolen items of nontrivial value without confrontation with the victim either within the home or outside the home (e.g., shoplifting, burglary, forgery).**

As a child or teenager, did you steal from stores, your parents, or other people?
   IF YES: What did you steal?
          How often did you steal?

Did you ever pick anyone's pocket, write a forged check, or use a credit card without permission?

(B11) **Has deliberately engaged in fire setting with the intention of causing serious damage.**

Did you ever set fires?
   IF YES: Why?

(B12) **Has deliberately destroyed other's property (other than by fire setting).**

Did you damage someone's property by breaking windows, spraying graffiti on walls, or other things like that?
   IF YES: What did you do?

(B13) **Has run away from home overnight at least twice while living in parental or parental surrogate home (or once without returning for a lengthy period).**

Did you ever run away from home overnight?
   IF YES: How often?
          How long did you stay away?

(B14) **Often truant from school, beginning before 13 years of age (for employed person, absent from work).**

Did you ever skip school?
   IF YES: How many times did you do it?
          Did you get into trouble for it?
          How old were you (in what grade were you) when you started to skip school?

(B15) Has broken into someone else's home, building, or car.

Did you ever break into anyone's house, a store, building or car?

C. A pervasive pattern of disregard for and violation of the rights of others occurring since age 15, as indicated by at least three of the following:

(C1) Failure to conform to social norms with respect to lawful behavior as indicated by repeatedly performing acts that are grounds for arrest.

I am not interested in knowing any specific details that might get you in trouble, but I need to ask how many times you might have done any of the following in the last five years:

_____ bought or sold stolen property
_____ embezzled other people's money
_____ ran numbers
_____ sold drugs
_____ shoplifted or stole things
_____ had sex for money
_____ did other things that could have gotten you arrested

Have you ever been arrested?
  IF YES: How many times?
          What were the circumstances?

(C2) Irritability and aggressiveness, as indicated by repeated physical fights or assaults.

How often have you been in physical fights?

What about attacking or hitting someone?

Have you ever been so angry that you started throwing things at your spouse/partner?
  IF YES: How often has this happened?

Have you ever spanked or hit a child hard enough so that he or she had bruises, had to stay in bed, or see a doctor?
  IF YES: How many times has this happened?

(C3) Consistent irresponsibility, as indicated by repeated failure to sustain consistent work behavior or honor financial obligations.

Have you sometimes been unable to pay for household necessities such as food, rent, or the electric bill because you spent so much money on things you could have done without?

Have you sometimes not paid bills or other financial obligations?
   IF YES: What were the circumstances?

Have you ever failed to make court ordered payments such as child support, alimony, or a lawsuit settlement?
   IF YES: Tell me about it.

When you have been working, have you ever gotten into trouble for not arriving on time, missing too many days, not doing your work, or not following the rules?
   IF YES: Tell me about that.

(C4) Impulsivity or failure to plan ahead.

How often have you just walked off a job or quit without any other work in sight? ("OTHER WORK" INCLUDES FULL-TIME STUDENT, HOMEMAKER, ETC.)
   IF PRESENT: Tell me about it.

How often have you impulsively picked up and moved around from place to place without any idea of how long you were going to stay or where you would go next?
   IF PRESENT: Tell me about it.

How often have you spent money impulsively on things you didn't need or couldn't afford?

Do you often get in trouble because you don't plan ahead?
   IF YES: Examples?

(C5) Deceitfulness, as indicated by repeated lying, use of aliases, or conning others for personal profit or pleasure.

Is it easy for you to lie if it serves your purpose?

Have you ever used a false name or developed a scheme to con people into giving you what you want?

(C6) Reckless disregard for safety of self or others.

How often have you been in auto accidents?
  IF MORE THAN ONE: How did they happen?

How often have you received speeding tickets or been charged with reckless driving?

What about driving while you were high on drugs or alcohol?

Are you known as someone who risks life and limb in recreational activities?
  IF YES: How did you get this reputation?
        IF NOT CLEARLY RECKLESS:
            Do you take all recommended safety precautions when doing these things?

Did you ever get into trouble at work for doing things that could be dangerous to you or others?
  IF YES: What happened?

(C7) Lack of remorse, as indicated by being indifferent to, or rationalizing having hurt, mistreated, or stolen from another.

You mentioned that you have (ANTISOCIAL BEHAVIOR(S) PREVIOUSLY DESCRIBED). How do you feel about that?
  IF NO REMORSE: Do you ever feel sorry or guilty?
              Do you think that [ANTISOCIAL BEHAVIOR] was justified?

(D) Exclude the diagnosis if the occurrence of antisocial behavior is exclusively during the course of schizophrenia or a manic episode.

NARCISSISTIC PD

Inclusion: At least 5 criteria
Exclusion: None

A pervasive pattern of grandiosity (in fantasy or behavior), need for admiration, and lack of empathy, beginning by early adulthood and present in a variety of contexts, as indicated by at least five of the following:

---

(1) **Has a grandiose sense of self-importance (e.g., exaggerates achievements and talents, expects to be recognized as superior without commensurate achievements).**

Would you describe yourself as someone who has or will accomplish great things--accomplishments that will set you apart from your equals?
   IF YES: Tell me about them.

Have people told you that you have too high an opinion of yourself?
   IF YES: Why do you think they said that?

---

(2) **Is preoccupied with fantasies of unlimited success, power, brilliance, beauty, or ideal love.**

When people imagine what their life would be like if they could have anything they want, they may think of such things as power, success, brilliance, beauty, the perfect relationship or other things. What do you daydream about? How often do you daydream about this?

Do your daydreams sometimes occupy your thoughts so much that it is hard to concentrate on your work or get things done?

How often do you feel bad or like a failure because you haven't achieved your dreams?

---

(3) **Believes that he or she is "special" and unique and can only be understood by, or should associate with, other special or high-status people (or institutions).**

Some people are so creative and unique that they have a hard time finding people like themselves to share things with. Does this sound like you?
 IF YES: What kind of person is able to understand you and be a good friend?

Do you consider yourself a particularly special or unique person?
 IF YES: In what way?
     Have you always felt this way about yourself?
     How has it affected how you relate to people?

Is it hard for others to understand you?
 IF YES: Why is that?

---

(4) **Requires excessive admiration.**

Is the praise and admiration of friends and colleagues important to you?
 IF YES: Do you often feel empty and hurt because people don't give you the praise and admiration you feel you deserve?

Has anyone ever accused you of fishing for compliments?

---

(5) **Has a sense of entitlement, i.e, unreasonable expectations of especially favorable treatment or automatic compliance with his or her expectations.**

Some people have earned the right to special consideration because of who they are or what they've done. Are there ways in which this applies to you?
 IF YES: Tell me about that.

Do you often get angry or irritated because you don't get the treatment you think you deserve?
 IF YES: Examples?
 IF NO: Has anyone else ever said that you acted this way?
     IF YES: What do you think made them say that?

Do you have a reputation for expecting others to do whatever you say without questioning it?

---

(6) **Is interpersonally exploitative, i.e., takes advantage of others to achieve his or her own ends.**

Are you pretty good at getting people to do what you want?
> IF YES: How do you get them to do what you want?
>> Do you ever pretend you're interested in someone so they'll do something for you?

Have you ever taken advantage of someone because it was the only way to get what you needed or deserved?
> IF YES: Can you describe a situation?
>> How often have you done something like this?

Do you have a reputation for doing whatever it takes to get what you want, even if it means stepping on other people?

---

(7) **Lacks empathy: is unwilling to recognize or identify with the feelings and needs of others.**

How do you feel when others start telling you about their problems?

Is it hard for you to put yourself in someone else's shoes and understand what they're going through?
> IF YES: Has this caused any problems for you?
>> Do you think you should try and understand?

Have other people complained that you are not very sympathetic to their problems?
> IF YES: Why do you think they said that?

---

(8) **Is often envious of others or believes that others are envious of him or her.**

Are there people you really envy or are jealous of?
> IF YES: What do you envy about them?
>> How often do you think about this?
>> Do you feel like you deserve what they have more than they do?
>> Does thinking about this bother you a lot or keep you from getting things done?

Are people often jealous or envious of you?
> IF YES: Why do you think they're jealous?

---

(9)   Shows arrogant, haughty behaviors or attitudes.

Have other people complained that you have an attitude problem?
  IF YES: What do they mean?
          What did they say?

(Has anyone ever said that you act as if you have a "chip on your shoulder?"
  IF YES: Why do you think they said that?)

Has anyone ever said that you act in an arrogant way?
  IF YES: Tell me about it.
          How often has this occurred?
          What problems has this caused?

(ALSO CONSIDER BEHAVIOR DURING INTERVIEW)

HISTRIONIC PD

Inclusion: At least 5 criteria
Exclusion: None

A pervasive pattern of excessive emotionality and attention seeking, beginning by early adulthood and present in a variety of contexts, as indicated by at least five of the following:

---

(1) **Is uncomfortable in situations in which he or she is not the center of attention.**

Some people prefer to be the center of attention while others are content to remain on the edge of things. Where would you put yourself?
   IF CENTER: How do you feel when you're not the center of attention?

Have other people said that you always need to be the center of attention?

---

(2) **Interaction with others is often characterized by inappropriate sexually seductive or provocative behavior.**

Do you have a reputation for being a flirt?
   IF YES: Tell me about that.

Do people sometimes misinterpret your friendliness as a romantic or sexual invitation?
   IF YES: How often does that happen?

(ALSO CONSIDER BEHAVIOR DURING INTERVIEW)

---

(3) **Displays rapidly shifting and shallow expression of emotions.**

Do your emotions and feelings change quickly?
   IF YES: Do other people notice?
      Have you always been like that?

Has anyone ever commented that your emotions do not seem real or sincere?
   IF YES: Tell me about that.

---

(4) Consistently uses physical appearance to draw attention to self.

Compared to other people your age, are you more interested in having your appearance noticed?

How often do you use your appearance to get people's attention?
IF OFTEN: How do you do that?

Are you disappointed when people don't notice how you look?

(ALSO CONSIDER APPEARANCE DURING INTERVIEW.)

---

(5) Has a style of speech that is excessively impressionistic and lacking in detail.

(***NOTE THROUGHOUT INTERVIEW WHETHER INDIVIDUAL IS ABLE TO GIVE CONCRETE EXAMPLES WITH APPROPRIATE DETAIL, ESPECIALLY WHEN (S)HE EXPRESSES A STRONG OPINION***)

---

(6) Shows self-dramatization, theatricality, and exaggerated expression of emotion.

Some people are very expressive. They cry at weddings, embrace people, show their fear and their joy. Would you say you are more or less likely than most people to show your emotions?
IF MORE: Has this ever caused you problems or embarrassment?

Has anyone ever said anything about how you show your emotions?
IF YES: What did they say?
         Do you agree?

Do you think you would make a good actor/actress?
IF YES: Why do you say that?

(ALSO CONSIDER EMOTIONAL EXPRESSIVITY DURING INTERVIEW)

---

(7) **Is suggestible, i.e., easily influenced by others or circumstances.**

Some people are so strongly influenced by others that they are easily swayed by their opinions. Do your opinions change easily depending on who you are with?
  IF YES: How often does this happen?

If someone says they have a problem such as a headache or upset stomach, or they feel some strong emotion, do you suddenly feel the same way?
  IF YES: Example?

---

(8) **Considers relationships to be more intimate than they actually are.**

Do you often feel a close bond to someone you have just met?
  IF YES: Does this happen a lot?
      Do you sometimes get hurt in relationships because you think the relationship is more serious than the other person does?

Are you quick to share personal details of your life with someone you have just met?
  IF YES: Can you think of times when this was a problem?

Do you often feel a close personal relationship with bosses or professionals you haven't known very long?

OBSESSIVE-COMPULSIVE PD

Inclusion: At least 4 criteria
Exclusion: None

A pervasive pattern of preoccupation with orderliness, perfectionism, and mental and interpersonal control, at the expense of flexibility, openness, and efficiency, beginning by early adulthood and present in a variety of contexts, as indicated by at least four of the following:

(1) Is preoccupied with details, rules, lists, order, organization, or schedules to the extent that the major point of the activity is lost.

Has anyone ever told you that you spend too much time making lists and schedules of what you need to do? Do you think you do?

When you have a task to do, do you often spend so much time getting organized that you have trouble getting the job done?

When you're working on something, do you often spend so much time on small details that you lose sight of the main thing you were trying to do?
   IF YES: Examples?

(2) Shows perfectionism that interferes with task completion (e.g., is unable to complete a project because his or her own overly strict standards are not met).

Would you say you are very perfectionistic?
Would others?
   IF YES TO EITHER: How often do your high standards keep you
                     from getting projects completed on time?
                     Examples?

---

(3) **Excessive devotion to work and productivity to the exclusion of leisure activities and friendships (not accounted for by obvious economic necessity).**

Would you call yourself a workaholic?
Have others said this about you?
  IF YES TO EITHER: Do you spend so much time working that you have little time for family activities, friendships, or entertainment?
  What about vacations?

Is it hard for you to enjoy a vacation because you're worried about getting behind in your work?
Do you usually take work along with you?

How many hours a week do you work?
  IF CONSIDERABLE: Why do you work so many hours?
  Would you still work that much if you could get the same pay for fewer hours?

---

(4) **Overconscientiousness, scrupulousness, and inflexibility about matters of morality, ethics, or values (not accounted for by cultural or religious identification).**

Do you have a strong sense of moral and ethical values?
  IF YES: Do you think you're more concerned about these values than most people you know?
  Would you have trouble being friends with someone who disagrees with you on moral or ethical issues?

How often do you worry that you've done something immoral or unethical?

Have other people complained that you are too strict about moral issues?
  IF YES: What did they complain about?

---

(5) **Is unable to discard worn-out or worthless objects even when they have no sentimental value.**

Some people find it impossible to throw anything away, even when it's old and worn out. Does this sound like you?
> **IF YES:** What kinds of things do you keep?
> Why do you keep them?
> Do others complain or tease you about the things you save?

---

(6) **Is reluctant to delegate tasks or to work with others unless they submit to exactly his or her way of doing things.**

Do you end up doing a lot of jobs yourself because you believe that no one else will do it exactly the way you want it done?
> **IF YES:** Examples?

Do you find yourself taking over other people's responsibilities to make sure that things get done right?
> **IF YES:** Examples?

---

(7) **Adopts a miserly spending style toward both self and others; money is viewed as something to be hoarded for future catastrophes.**

After you pay your bills, what kinds of things do you like to spend money on?

Are you slow to spend money on yourself? How about spending money on others?

Some people worry so much about something terrible happening in the future that they save all their money to be prepared for that future catastrophe. Does this sound like you?
> **IF YES:** Tell me about that.

---

(8) **Shows rigidity and stubbornness.**

Would other people describe you as being stubborn or set in your ways? What about inflexible or closed-minded?
> **IF YES:** What makes them say that?
> Do you agree?

AVOIDANT PD

Inclusion: At least 4 criteria
Exclusion: None

A pervasive pattern of social inhibition, feelings of inadequacy, and hypersensitivity to negative evaluation, beginning by early adulthood and present in a variety of contexts, as indicated by at least four of the following:

---

(1) Avoids occupational activities that involve significant interpersonal contact, because of fears of criticism, disapproval, or rejection.

Do you try to avoid the kind of work that requires a lot of contact with people or do you enjoy that kind of work?
IF AVOIDS: Why is that?
　　　　　　　IF UNCLEAR: Are you afraid that people will criticize or reject you?

Have you ever turned down a job or promotion because it would have required more contact with people?
IF YES: Why is that?

---

(2) Is unwilling to get involved with people unless certain of being liked.

How often do you avoid getting to know someone because you are worried they may not like you?
IF OFTEN: Has this affected the number of friends you have?

---

(3) Shows restraint within intimate relationships because of the fear of being shamed or ridiculed.

Even when you're in a close relationship, do you often keep your thoughts and feelings to yourself because you're afraid the other person might put you down?
IF YES: How much has this fear kept you from feeling really comfortable in close relationships?

---

(4) Is preoccupied with being criticized or rejected in social situations.

In social situations, how much do you worry about being criticized or rejected by other people?

Do you worry about rejection?
   IF YES: Tell me about it.
            How does this concern affect your behavior?

If you are criticized, would you think about it for hours or even days?

---

(5) Is inhibited in new interpersonal situations because of feelings of inadequacy.

Do you have a lot more trouble than most people carrying on a conversation with someone you've just met?
   IF YES: What makes it hard?

Do you often feel inadequate in social situations?
   IF YES: How much does this get in the way of your meeting new people and making friends?

---

(6) Views self as socially inept, personally unappealing, or inferior to others.

Do you usually feel like you're not as interesting or fun as other people?

How do you think you relate to people in social situations?
   IF POOR: Why do you think that is?

---

(7) Is unusually reluctant to take personal risks or to engage in any new activities because they may prove embarrassing.

Some people are willing to take some risks or take on new activities, whereas others always play it safe. How would you describe yourself?

How often do you avoid taking chances or trying new activities because you're worried about embarrassing yourself?
   IF OFTEN: Examples?

DEPENDENT PD

Inclusion: At least 5 criteria
Exclusion: None

A pervasive and excessive need to be taken care of that leads to submissive and clinging behavior and fears of separation, beginning by early adulthood and present in a variety of contexts, as indicated by at least five of the following:

---

(1) Has difficulty making everyday decisions without an excessive amount of advice and reassurance from others.

Some people enjoy making decisions and other people prefer to have someone they trust tell them what to do. Which do you prefer?

How much do you look for reassurance or advice about everyday decisions like what to have for lunch or what clothes to buy? Is it difficult for you to make these kinds of decisions on your own?

---

(2) Needs others to assume responsibility for most major areas of his or her life.

Some people often end up in situations where other people make decisions about important areas of their life. For example, they let someone else decide whether they should take a job, who their friends should be, etc. Does this sound like your life?
  IF YES: What keeps you from making decisions on your own?

---

(3) Has difficulty expressing disagreement with others because of fear of loss of support or approval (NOTE: Do not include realistic fears of retribution).

How hard is it for you to express a different opinion with someone you're close to?
  IF HARD: What do you worry might happen if you do?

Do you often pretend to agree with others so they won't reject you or dislike you?

(4) **Has difficulty initiating projects or doing things on his or her own (because of a lack of self-confidence in judgement or abilities rather than a lack of motivation or energy).**

Do you usually need help from somebody else to get started on a project or do things on your own?
   IF YES: Why is that? Is it because you don't feel confident about your own abilities?

(5) **Goes to excessive lengths to obtain nurturance and support from others, to the point of volunteering to do things that are unpleasant.**

Do you bend over backwards to do things for others just so they'll take care of you when you need it?
   IF YES: Do you ever volunteer to do unpleasant things for this reason? Examples?

(6) **Feels uncomfortable or helpless when alone, because of exaggerated fears of being unable to care for himself or herself.**

How do you usually feel when you're alone?
   IF UNCOMFORTABLE: Are you often afraid that you won't be able to take care of yourself?
      IF YES: In what way?

(7) **Urgently seeks another relationship as a source of care and support when a close relationship ends.**

What do you do when a close relationship ends? Would you be desperate to get into another relationship right away even if it was not the best person for you? **IF YES:** Why is that?

(8) **Is unrealistically preoccupied with fears of being left to take care of himself or herself.**

How much do you worry about people you depend on leaving you?
   IF WORRIES: What has caused your concern?
      Are there times when you can't stop worrying about this?
      Are you worried that you won't be able to take care of yourself?

THE MENTAL STATUS EXAMINATION (MSE)

The mental status examination is analogous to the physical examination. The focus is on <u>current</u> signs, symptoms, affect, behavior, and cognition. Some excellent books and book chapters have been written about the mental status exam; however, students and beginning clinicians usually condense these texts to an outline which they follow when writing up the mental status part of the psychiatric evaluation. Below is such an outline.

The outline represents a standardized way of presenting (orally or in writing) the mental status exam. This outline should not be used as a checklist of items to ask of the patients, and should not influence the flow of the psychiatric interview. The best interviewers let the patient do most of the talking (at least at the beginning of the evaluation), and they follow the patient's lead in collecting the mental status exam data base. This differs from the detailed physical exam, in which the order of the exam is often the same for all patients (e.g., start at the head and work downwards).

A good interviewer is not just listening to the content of the patient's speech. He or she is also observing affect and motor behavior, monitoring the amount, flow and quality of speech, and noting whether the connections between words, phrases, and sentences deviates from normal goal directed speech.

Authors vary in how they delineate the sections of the mental status exam. The outline below consists of 10 sections, with multiple components to each. For many of the components, I have included lists of frequently used descriptors. The list is <u>not</u> exhaustive.

A short glossary defining some of the terms that cause the greatest confusion follows the outline. The glossary is arranged in alphabetical order. In parentheses after each term is the section of the mental status examination where the term is used.

MENTAL STATUS EXAMINATION OUTLINE

APPEARANCE: Age (chronological age and whether person looks this
age)
Sex, Race
Body build (thin, obese, cachectic, muscular, frail,
medium)
Position (lying, sitting, standing, kneeling)
Posture (rigid, slumped, cross-legged, slouched,
comfortable, threatening)
Eye contact
Dress (what individual is wearing, cleanliness, condition
of clothes, neatness, appropriateness of garments)
Grooming (malodorous, highly perfumed, dirty, unshaven,
kemptness, smelling of alcohol, hairstyle, makeup)
Manner (cooperativeness, guarded, pleasant, suspicious,
glib, angry, seductive, ingratiating, evasive, friendly,
inappropriately familiar, hostile)
Attentiveness to examiner (disinterested, bored,
internally preoccupied, distractible, attentive)
Distinguishing features (scars, tattoos, bandages, blood
stains, missing teeth, tobacco stained fingers)
Prominent physical abnormalities (missing limb, jaundice,
profuse sweating, goiter, wheezing, coughing)
Emotional facial expression (crying, screaming,
tremulous, looking upward as if hearing voices,
perspiring, furrowed brow, sitting calmly)
Alertness (alert, drowsy, stupor, comatose)

MOTOR: Retardation (slowed movements)
Agitation (unable to sit still, wringing hands, rocking,
picking at skin or clothing, pacing)
Abnormal movements (tremor, lip smacking, tongue
thrust, mannerisms, grimaces, tics)
Gait (shuffling, broad based, limping, stumbling,
festinating)
Catatonia (stupor, excitement, waxy flexibility)

SPEECH: Rate (slowed, long pauses before answering questions,
hesitant, rapid, pressured)
Rhythm (monotonous, stuttering)
Volume (loud, soft, whispered)
Amount (monosyllabic, hypertalkative, mute)
Articulation (clear, mumbled, slurred, dysarthric)
Spontaneity

AFFECT:
Stability (stable, fixed, labile)
Range (constricted, full)
Appropriateness (to content of speech and circumstances)
Intensity (flat, blunted, exaggerated)
Affect (depressed, sad, happy, euphoric, irritable, anxious, neutral, fearful, angry, apathetic, pleasant)
Mood (patient's report)

THOUGHT CONTENT:
Suicidal ideation
Death wishes
Homicidal ideation
Depressive cognitions (guilt, worthless, hopeless)
Obsessions
Ruminations
Phobias
Ideas of reference
Paranoid ideation
Magical ideation
Delusions
Overvalued ideas
Other major themes discussed by patient

THOUGHT PROCESS:
Associations
Coherence (coherent, incoherent)
Logic (logical, illogical)
Stream (goal directed, circumstantial, tangential, loose, flight of ideas, rambling, word salad)
Clang associations
Perseverative
Neologism
Blocking
Attention (distractibility, concentration)

PERCEPTION:
Hallucinations (auditory, visual, olfactory, gustatory, tactile)
Illusions
Depersonalization
Derealization
Deja vu, Jamais vu

INTELLECT:
Global evaluation (average, above or below average)

INSIGHT:
Awareness of illness

MINI-MENTAL STATE EXAM: (see next page)

MINI-MENTAL STATE EXAMINATION

The Mini-Mental State Examination (MMSE, Folstein et al, 1975) is the most widely used screening evaluation for cognitive impairment. The MMSE has been used to screen for dementia and delirium, grossly quantify the degree of cognitive impairment, and serially measure cognitive changes over time. It should be emphasized that the MMSE is only a screening measure, and it should not be used as the sole criterion for diagnosing dementia.

The MMSE is reprinted on the next two pages. Scores range from 0-30, and values of 23 or less suggest the presence of cognitive impairment. Some authorities recommend that three levels of cognitive impairment be delineated: 24-30 = no cognitive impairment; 18-23 = mild cognitive impairment; and 0-17 = severe cognitive impairment. MMSE scores are correlated with years of education, and the established cutoff points are probably not valid if the patient has less than a ninth grade education.

The MMSE has been reprinted with permission from: Folstein MF, Folstein SE, and McHugh PR. "Mini-mental State:" A practical method for grading the cognitive states of patients for the clinician. *Journal of Psychiatric Research*, 1975, *12*: 189-198.

MINI-MENTAL STATE EXAM (Folstein)

Now I'm going to ask you some questions to test your concentration and memory.

ORIENTATION TO TIME
( ) What year is this? [1 point]
( ) What season of the year is it? [1 point]
( ) What is the month and date? [1 point for each]
( ) What day of the week is it? [1 point]

ORIENTATION TO PLACE
( ) What is the name of this place? [1 point]
( ) What floor are we on? [1 point]
( ) What city and state are we in? [1 point for each]
( ) What county is this? [1 point]

IMMEDIATE RECALL
( ) I am going to say 3 objects. After I say them, I want you to repeat them. They are: "Apple" "Table" "Penny." Now you say them. Remember what they are because I'm going to ask you to name them again in a few minutes. [1 point for each]
(Interviewer: Repeat until all 3 are learned.)

ATTENTION (either item)
( ) a) Subtract 7 from 100, then subtract 7 from the answer you get and keep subtracting 7 until I tell you to stop. [1 point for each correct answer, maximum 5 points]
b) Spell the word "world" backwards. [1 point for each correct letter, maximum 5 points]

DELAYED RECALL
( ) What are the 3 words I asked you to remember? [1 for each]

NAMING
( ) Show patient wrist watch and pen and ask to name them. [1 point for each]

REPETITION
( ) Repeat the following sentence exactly as I say it. "No ifs, ands, or buts." [1 point]

3 STAGE COMMAND
( ) Now I want to see how well you can follow instructions. I'm going to give you a piece of paper. Take it in your right hand, use both hands to fold it in half, and then put it on the floor. [1 point for each command, maximum 3 points]

READING
( ) Show patient page 125 and ask patient to read what it says at the top of the page silently, to him/herself, and then do what it says. [1 point]

COPYING
( ) Give patient clean sheet of paper and ask him/her to copy the design printed on page 125. [1 point]

WRITING
( ) On same sheet of paper, ask patient to write a complete sentence. [1 point]

( ) **Total** (Maximum score = 30)

CLOSE YOUR EYES

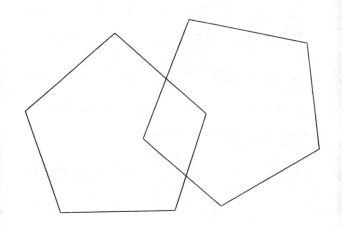

GLOSSARY OF TERMS

<u>Affect</u> The observed emotional state during the evaluation.

    1. <u>Blunted affect</u> refers to minimal expression and intensity of emotion. The individual's facial expression varies little. There are few physical gestures of emotion, eye contact is either minimal or the patient seems to stare at the interviewer, and the patient speaks in a monotonous tone with little vocal inflection. The person's face seems to have little muscle tone.

    2. <u>Constricted affect</u> refers to a limited range of expressed emotion. The emotion may be intense (severe depression, anger), but there is little variability of expression during the interview.

    3. <u>Flat affect</u> is a more severe form of blunted affect with essentially no affective expression. The interviewer may feel as if he or she is conversing with an inanimate object.

    4. <u>Inappropriate affect</u> refers to a discordance between the content of speech and the expressed emotion (e.g., laughing while discussing the death of a loved one).

    5. <u>Labile affect</u> refers to abrupt, rapid, and repeated shifts of type and intensity of emotion.

<u>Alexithymia</u> (affect) Impaired ability to recognize subjective mood state and to describe emotions verbally.

<u>Circumstantiality</u> (thought process) Speech that takes a circuitous route before reaching its goal. Extra, unnecessary, and sometimes tedious details are added. The speaker often needs to be interrupted. However, there is a clearly recognized link between the associations (in contrast to looseness of associations).

<u>Clang Associations</u> (thought process) Speech in which the sounds of words, rather than their meaning, guide the choice of words. Puns and rhymes are characteristic. (e.g., "Where should I lie? If I lie, will I die? Go to the sky, way up high?")

<u>Delusion</u> (thought content) A fixed, false belief that is not shared with members of the individual's culture or religion. The distinction between a delusional and a false nondelusional idea is not always clearcut. For example, a clinically depressed president of a corporation who feels like a failure and a disappointment to his/her family and friends would usually not be considered delusional unless he or she claimed to be poverty stricken (despite a sizable bank account), or responsible for causing tragic

events to which he or she has no connection. The obsessions of some individuals with obsessive compulsive disorder are firmly held, and only after considerable discussion do they acknowledge that the belief may be incorrect. Underweight anorexics may incorrectly believe they are fat; however, this is usually not considered a delusion. The content of most delusions fall into one of the following 14 categories:

1. <u>Delusion of control.</u> Delusional belief that one's actions, behavior, or feelings are not under personal control or own doing, but are imposed by an external force. The essential requirement is that the individual believes his will, thoughts or feelings have been replaced by something external (e.g., "The spirit of my dead father is inside me and controls me.")

2. <u>Delusion of guilt or sin.</u> Delusional belief of responsibility for tragedy or disaster to which there is no personal connection (e.g., "The Persian Gulf war was my fault."). Delusional belief of having done something terrible and now must face deserved retribution or punishment.

3. <u>Delusion of grandiosity.</u> Delusional belief of special power, talent, abilities, or identity. (e.g., Individuals who believe they are Christ, an apostle, Hitler, Elvis, etc. Patient believed he was responsible for the Camp David accord between Israel and Egypt, and now was needed in the Middle East to help settle the Palestinian problem).

4. <u>Delusion of jealousy.</u> With little or no evidence, the person believes one's sexual partner is unfaithful. The person often goes to great effort to prove the existence of the affair. (e.g., A patient attempted to remain awake all night to catch his wife sneaking out of the house. He attached a string from her toe to his. He asserted that after he fell asleep at approximately 4 a.m., his wife slipped off the string, left the house to participate in an orgy, and returned to reattach the string before he awakened. The patient was referred to psychiatry after he brought his wife's panties to the OB-GYN department requesting an examination and analysis of semen residue.)

5. <u>Delusion of mind reading.</u> Delusional belief that people can read one's mind or know one's thoughts. This does not include sensing what a person is thinking by body language or facial expression. It also differs from thought broadcasting (see below), in that the patient does not believe that his thoughts are heard by others.

6. <u>Delusion of persecution.</u> Delusional belief that one is in danger, being followed or monitored, harassed, or conspired against. This may involve government agencies (FBI, police), criminal groups (the mob, mafia, drug dealers), neighbors, coworkers, and even family.

7. <u>Delusion of reference.</u>   Delusional belief that ordinary, insignificant comments, objects, or events refer to or have special meaning for the patient. (e.g., Patient believed that songs on the radio had subliminal messages intended specifically for him.)

8. <u>Delusion of replacement.</u>   Delusional belief that someone important to the patient (e.g., family member, spouse) has been replaced by a double. Also called Doppelganger.

9. <u>Erotomania.</u> Delusional belief that one is loved, perhaps secretly, by another person. Usually the other person is of higher status than the patient.

10. <u>Nihilistic delusion.</u> Delusional belief that the person, a part of the person's body, or the world does not exist. (e.g., "Aliens took my brain out of my head and put it in the drawer of the desk. I no longer have a brain.")

11. <u>Somatic delusion.</u> Delusional belief that one's body is diseased or changed. (e.g., A depressed man with constipation believed he had colon cancer despite a negative GI work-up. Another male patient believed he was pregnant.)

12. <u>Thought broadcasting.</u> Delusional belief that as thoughts occur, they escape from the person's head and can be heard by others. The patient may or may not also hear his thoughts aloud. (e.g., A patient believed that the FBI was tape recording his thoughts, even though he wasn't speaking.)

13. <u>Thought insertion.</u> Delusional belief that thoughts are not one's own, but have been placed there by some person, group, or force from the outside. (e.g., During an interview the patient uttered an obscenity, turned towards a group of patients behind him, and emphatically said to the interviewer that they put that word into his head because he never curses.)

14. <u>Thought withdrawal.</u> Delusional belief that one's thoughts have been removed or taken away by someone or something from the outside.

<u>**Deja Vu**</u> (perception) The feeling that one has already experienced a particular moment or event before.

<u>**Depersonalization**</u> (perception) An altered sense of one's physical being. Includes feeling outside of one's body, physically cut off or distanced from people, floating, observing oneself from a distance, like one is in a dream, or that one's body is physically changed in shape or size.

Derealization (perception) A sense that one's environment has changed and is different than the way it had been before, though the individual cannot identify tangible elements of change.

Distractibility (thought process) Attention to the interviewer is easily disrupted by unimportant external stimuli.

Flight of Ideas (thought process) Rapid speech with abrupt changes from topic to topic usually based on understandable links between the topics, distracting external stimuli, or plays on words. When severe, the link between the associations may be so obscure that loosening of associations or incoherence may also be present (see definitions below).

Hallucinations (perception) A sensory perception in the absence of an actual external stimulus. They can occur in any sensory system of the body: sight, hearing, taste, smell, and touch.

    1. _Auditory hallucination._ Usually refers to hearing voices, but also can refer to hearing noises, sounds, music, etc.

    2. _Hypnogogic hallucination._ Occurs when an individual is falling asleep and is considered a pseudo-hallucination. It has significance only for the diagnosis of abnormal sleep states, and is not indicative of psychopathology.

    3. _Hypnopompic hallucination._ Is analogous to a hypnogogic hallucination, except it occurs upon awakening.

    4. _Olfactory hallucination._ A hallucination involving smell. Of note, the belief that one has a noxious or peculiar body odor is not a hallucination unless the person also smells it.

    5. _Tactile hallucination._ A hallucination involving the sense of touch.

    6. _Visual hallucination._ Usually refers to seeing people or animals that are not actually there, but also can refer to seeing shapes, colors, flashes of light, etc.

Idea of Reference (thought content) Similar to a delusion of reference except the person questions the reality of the belief. (e.g., A patient wondered whether everyone on the bus was talking about him, but knew this was unlikely to be true.)

Illogical Thinking (thought process) Thinking that contains clear internal contradictions, or in which conclusions are reached which make no logical sense. (e.g., "My mother died before I was born.")

Illusion (perception)   A misperception of a real external stimulus. This is distinguished from a hallucination which is the perception of a non-existent external stimulus (e.g., Misinterpretation of shadows as people, or noises as people's voices.)

Jamais Vu (perception)   The feeling of unfamiliarity with familiar situations.

Incoherence (thought process)   Incomprehensible speech due to disruption of logical or meaningful connection between words or phrases, many incomplete sentences, idiosyncratic use of words, and distorted grammar.

Looseness of Associations   (thought process)   Speech characterized by a disruption of logical or meaningful connection between the ideas and thoughts in the sequence. Sometimes there is an oblique association between ideas, sometimes there is no association at all. The individual is unaware of the lack of connectedness between the thoughts. Often the interviewer will be left wondering what the patient just said.

Magical Thinking (thought content)   The belief that thinking something will cause it to occur. This is normal in children (e.g., children avoiding stepping on a sidewalk crack so they won't "break their mother's back").

Mood (affect)   The sustained emotion experienced and reported by an individual. This contrasts to affect, which is the emotional tone perceived by an observer.

Neologism (thought process)   A new word, distortion of words, or condensed combination of words created by the patient, and which has a specific meaning to the patient. (e.g., "I futiligated the rocket to outer space.")

Nonsequitur (thought process)   A response that does not follow from the question asked. Often used by politicians. (e.g., "Where were you born?" "I'm not sure if that's the way it's always been or not.")

Overvalued Idea (thought content)   A relatively firmly held false belief that is not shared with members of the individual's culture or religion, but which is not maintained with delusional intensity. (e.g., A patient who is concerned about getting AIDS from a public toilet seat acknowledges he may be wrong but still wants an HIV blood test.)

Perseveration   (thought process)   Repetition of the same word, phrase, or idea in response to different questions. This does not include the use of filler words such as "you know," "like," or "I mean." (e.g., That's my story. Things happen and this is how my story unfolded. My story isn't a happy one, and I hope my story for the future will be better.)

Preoccupation (thought process) Mental absorption in a particular topic or concern.

Pressured Speech (speech) Rapid, continuous speech that is difficult to interrupt.

Psychosis A severe mental disturbance indicating gross impairment in reality testing. Manifestations of psychosis include delusions, hallucinations, looseness of associations, grossly disorganized and bizarre speech or behavior.

Rambling (thought process) Speech that is fragmented, without goal, and usually associated with intoxication.

Tangentiality (thought process) Speech that talks past the point, and never reaches the goal of answering the question. Similar to circumstantial speech, but in contrast to looseness of associations, there is a clearly recognized link between associations. In contrast to circumstantial speech the goal is never reached.

Thought Blocking (thought process) A sudden interruption in the spontaneous flow of speech associated with the person saying that his mind went blank. Upon questioning, after a period of silence, the individual states he cannot recall what he was talking about.

Thought Disorder (thought process) Also referred to as formal thought disorder. A generic term that refers to abnormalities in the form of thought in contrast to the content of thought.

Word Salad (thought process) Speech that is incomprehensible and incoherent because of a lack of logical and meaningful connection between words. It represents the exteme form of looseness of associations.

BRIEF PSYCHOSOCIAL HISTORY

Now, I'd like to ask you some questions about your childhood and some other areas of your life.

CHILDHOOD

Where were you born and raised?
   (When did you move?) (Why did you move?)
Were your parents married?
Did your mother have problems with the pregnancy or delivery?
Did you reach your developmental milestones, like walking, talking, potty training, on time?

With whom did you live while you were growing up?
Who did you feel closest to?
Who in the family was affectionate to you?
How did you get along with [PERSONS RAISING PATIENT]?

Who made the rules and enforced discipline?
Were the family rules pretty clear and consistently applied?
Do you think the rules were fair?
How often did you get punished?
How did they usually discipline you?
Did they ever spank or hit you?
   IF YES: Did they ever leave bruises when they hit you?
            Did you ever have to see a doctor?

Did you see violence in the family?
Did anyone sexually abuse you?
   IF YES: What happened?
            How often did it occur?
            How much did this upset you at the time?
            What about now?

At what age did you begin school?
Did you go to regular or special classes?
   IF SPECIAL CLASSES: Why?
How did you do in school? (What were your grades?)
Did you ever repeat a grade?
What was the last grade you completed?
Were you involved in school activities? **IF YES:** Like what?
What did you do after you graduated (or dropped out)?

What was your personality like as a child?
Did you have many friends as a child?
   (Did you have any really close friends? Best friends?)
Were you more of a leader or a follower?

PARENTHOOD

Do you have any children?
> **IF YES:** How many? What are their ages and sexes?
> How do you get along with them?

FRIENDSHIPS AND MARRIAGE

Do you have many friends now?
> (Any close friends, that is, someone you can really trust with secrets?)
> (Do you tend to keep friends for a long time?)

Have you ever been married?
> **IF YES:** How many times?
> How would you describe your marriage(s)?
> > **IF DIVORCED:** Why did you divorce?
> **IF NO:** How come you never got married?

Almost all couples argue or fight, and I'd like to know a little bit about what happens when you and your partner have disagreements. Do you or your partner ever get pushed, grabbed, or hit during these times? What about throwing things?
> **IF YES:** Describe the most recent (or serious) time that this happened.
> How often does something like this happen?
> Have you ever had to go to a doctor because of injuries received during a fight?
> **IF NO:** Did this ever happen in prior relationships? (Tell me about it.)
> Are you ever afraid that you will be physically hurt during or after an argument with your (SPOUSE, BOY/GIRLFRIEND)?

OCCUPATION

Are you employed?
> **IF YES:** What kind of work do you do?
> How long have you worked there? Do you like it?
> What other jobs have you had? Why did you leave?
> What's the longest job you've ever had?
> **IF NO:** When was the last time you worked? What happened?
> What kind of job was it?
> What other jobs have you had?
> What's the longest job you've ever had?

LIVING SITUATION

Where do you live?
Do you live in an apartment? A house?
How long have you been living there?
> (Where did you previously live?)
> (Why did you move?) (Have you moved much?)
> (Have you ever not had a place to stay? What did you do?)
With whom do you live?

CURRENT PSYCHOSOCIAL FUNCTIONING

Employment

Do you work?
  IF YES:

> What kind of work do you do?
> How many hours per week do you work?
> Did you miss any time from work during the past week?
> > **IF YES:** How much time did you miss?
> > For what reason?
>
> Did you have any problems on the job during the past week?
> > **IF YES:** Like what?
>
> Does anyone evaluate your performance at work? **IF YES:** Who?
> Does anyone (else) give you feedback on your performance?
> **IF YES:** Who?
> > **IF YES TO EITHER:**
> > What do they look at to determine whether you're doing a good job?
> > What kind of evaluations have you gotten?
> > What do <u>you</u> look at to determine if you're doing a good job?
> > How well did you do your job during the past week?
> > Could you give me some examples?
>
> > **IF NO TO BOTH:**
> > What do <u>you</u> look at to determine if you're doing a good job?
> > How well did you do your job during the past week?
> > Could you give me some examples?
>
> **IF NOT ALREADY CLEAR FROM ABOVE:**
> In what way did your (PATIENT DESCRIPTION OF HEALTH PROBLEM) effect your job during the past week?
> Because of your (HEALTH PROBLEM), were there things you didn't get done at work?
> > **IF YES:** Like what?
>
> Did your (HEALTH PROBLEM) cause problems concentrating at work?
> Did you work as efficiently as usual?
> > **IF NO:** Describe that for me.

IF NO: Why didn't you work this past week?

Household work

What responsibilities do you have in your household?
Do you do any cleaning?
Laundry?
Cooking?
Shopping?
House repairs or yard work?
Take care of any kids or older or disabled family members?
Run errands?
Is there anything else that you do to keep your household running?

During this past week how well have you been keeping up with your household responsibilities?

Are there any things you usually do that you didn't get done this past week?
   IF YES: What kept you from (TASK)?
                 Were there days you didn't get anything done?
                    IF YES: How many days were like that?

Did you have any difficulty doing your household chores?
   IF YES: Like what?

How would you rate your performance of household chores for the past week?
Can you give me some examples?

IF NOT ALREADY CLEAR FROM ABOVE:
   In what way did your (HEALTH PROBLEM) affect your (SPECIFIC CHORES)?
   Because of (HEALTH PROBLEM), were there things you didn't get done?
      IF YES: Like what?
   Were there things you didn't do as well as usual?
      IF YES: Like what?

Schoolwork

Do you go to school or take any classes?
>   **IF YES:**   Are you a full-time student?
>>   **IF NO:**   How many classes do you take?

ASK THE FOLLOWING IF AT LEAST A HALF-TIME STUDENT

Did you miss or skip any classes this past week?
>   **IF YES:**   How many?
>   For what reason?

Were you given any assignments, homework, or tests this past week?
>   **IF YES:**   How did you do?
>>   **IF UNSURE:**   How do you think you did? (How do you usually do?)

How have your study habits been this past week?

IF EVIDENCE OF IMPAIRED FUNCTIONING:
Were there days you didn't get anything done? That is, you couldn't go to classes or you couldn't do any homework or studying?
>   **IF YES:**   How many days were like that?

IF NOT ALREADY CLEAR FROM ABOVE:
How did your (HEALTH PROBLEM) specifically affect your schoolwork this past week?
Did your (HEALTH PROBLEM) cause problems concentrating?
Did you work as efficiently as usual?
>   **IF NO:** Describe that for me.

Relationships with husband, wife, boyfriend, girlfriend, or lover

Are you married?

    IF YES: How would you describe your marriage?

              How close a relationship do you and your spouse usually have?

              How were things this past week?

              Did you have any arguments or disagreements this past week?

              IF YES: How often did you argue?

                        For how long did you stay angry at each other?

                        Were you able to work out your problems?

    IF NO: Do you have a boyfriend or girlfriend or lover?

              IF YES: How long have you been going with him/her?

                        Do you live together?

                        How close a relationship do you and your partner usually have?

                        How have you gotten along this past week?

                        Did you have any arguments or disagreements this past week?

                        IF YES: How often did you argue?

                                  For how long did you stay angry at each other?

                                Were you able to work out your problems?

IF NOT ALREADY CLEAR FROM ABOVE:

    How did your (HEALTH PROBLEM) affect your relationship?

    Did it affect your closeness?

    Have you been more withdrawn?

    Did you argue more or less?

Relationships with other family members

Who is in your immediate family? Your extended family? Do you have
in-laws? Grandparents? Grandchildren? Any other family?

Are your parents still alive?
    IF YES: Are you close?
                How do you get along with them?
                Did you see or speak to them this past week?
                How have you gotten along with them this past week?
                Did you have any arguments or disagreements this past
                week?
                IF YES: How often did you argue?
                              For how long did you stay angry at each other?

Do you have any brothers or sisters?
    IF YES: Are you close?
                How do you get along with them?
                Did you see or speak to them this past week?
                How have you gotten along with them this past week?
                Did you have any arguments or disagreements this past
                week?
                IF YES: How often did you argue?
                              For how long did you stay angry at each other?

Do you have any children?
    IF YES: Are you close?
                How old are they?
                Did you see or speak to them this past week?
                How have you gotten along with them this past week?
                Did you have any arguments or disagreements this past
                week?
                IF YES: How often did you argue?
                              For how long did you stay angry at each other?

Are there family members that you avoid seeing because of serious
problems or trouble getting along?

IF NOT ALREADY CLEAR:
    How did your (HEALTH PROBLEM) affect your relationships with your
    family?
    Did it effect your closeness with anyone?
    Have you been more withdrawn?
    Did you argue more or less with anyone?

Relationships with friends

Not counting your family members, do you have any close friends you can confide in about a personal matter?

IF YES: How many close friends do you have?

How often do you usually see or speak to them?

What about this past week?

How have you been getting along with them over the past week?

Any arguments or disagreements?

How strong are the ties between you?

IF NO: How many people do you know that you wouldn't necessarily confide in, but whom you would consider friends?

IF ONE OR MORE:

How often do you usually see or speak to them?

What about this past week?

How have you been getting along with your friends over the past week?

Any arguments or disagreements?

How strong are the ties between you?

IF NOT ALREADY CLEAR:

How did your (HEALTH PROBLEM) effect your relationships with your friends?

Did it effect your closeness with anyone?

Have you been more withdrawn?

Did you argue more or less with anyone because of your (HEALTH PROBLEM)?

Recreation

What kinds of leisure or recreational activities do you enjoy?
Do you have any hobbies?
(Are there any activities [outside of work] that you do regularly or occasionally?)
What did you do for fun this past week?

What about: reading?
               watching or playing sports?
               participating in community groups?
               exercising?
               gardening?
               going to the movies, plays or concerts?
               crafts?
               watching television?
               listening to or playing music?
               going to church, synagogue or temple?
               hobbies?
               parties?

How often did you (ACTIVITY MENTIONED ABOVE)?

How much did you enjoy (ACTIVITY)?

How much did your (HEALTH PROBLEM) affect your participation in leisure, recreational and fun activities?

How much did your (HEALTH PROBLEM) affect your enjoyment of the things you did?

General satisfaction with life

We've reviewed several areas of your life - work, housework, relationships with family and friends, and leisure. The last thing I'd like to ask you about is your level of satisfaction with your life. Considering all the different areas of your life, how satisfied overall have you felt about your life during the past week?

IF GENERALLY SATISFIED:

Are you satisfied with all areas of your life?

IF NO: Which areas are you dissatisfied with?

How dissatisfied are you?

IF YES: Any dissatisfaction in any areas?

IF YES: Which ones?

How dissatisfied are you?

IF GENERALLY DISSATISFIED:

Are you dissatisfied with all areas of your life?

IF NO: Which areas are you satisfied with?

How satisfied are you?

IF YES: Any satisfaction in any area?

IF YES: Which ones?

How satisfied are you?

ORDERING INFORMATION

Title: Interview Guide for Evaluating DSM-IV Psychiatric Disorders and
the Mental Status Examination   ISBN: 0-9633821-3-6

PRICE LIST

# copies	Cost
1-4	$11.00 (plus $3.50 Shipping & Handling [S/H]) = $14.50/copy
5-24	$11.00/copy (S/H included)
25-100 [18% off]	$9.00/copy (S/H included)
> 100	Call for price quote

All orders will be shipped via UPS. Prepayment by check or money order
is necessary.

Payable to: Psych Products Press

Mailing address: Psych Products Press
P.O. Box 228
East Greenwich, RI 02818

Phone: (401) 885-6746

Shipping address: _____

_____

_____

_____